Shock!

A Thriller

Brian Clemens

A Samuel French Acting Edition

SAMUELFRENCH-LONDON.CO.UK
SAMUELFRENCH.COM

Copyright © 1979 by Clemens Enterprisees Ltd
All Rights Reserved

SHOCK! is fully protected under the copyright laws of the British Commonwealth, including Canada, the United States of America, and all other countries of the Copyright Union. All rights, including professional and amateur stage productions, recitation, lecturing, public reading, motion picture, radio broadcasting, television and the rights of translation into foreign languages are strictly reserved.

ISBN 978-0-573-11410-6

www.samuelfrench-london.co.uk

www.samuelfrench.com

FOR AMATEUR PRODUCTION ENQUIRIES

UNITED KINGDOM AND WORLD EXCLUDING NORTH AMERICA

plays@SamuelFrench-London.co.uk

020 7255 4302/01

Each title is subject to availability from Samuel French, depending upon country of performance.

CAUTION: Professional and amateur producers are hereby warned that *SHOCK!* is subject to a licensing fee. Publication of this play does not imply availability for performance. Both amateurs and professionals considering a production are strongly advised to apply to the appropriate agent before starting rehearsals, advertising, or booking a theatre. A licensing fee must be paid whether the title is presented for charity or gain and whether or not admission is charged.

The professional rights in this play are controlled by Samuel French Ltd, 52 Fitzroy Street, London, W1T 5JR.

No one shall make any changes in this title for the purpose of production. No part of this book may be reproduced, stored in a retrieval system, or transmitted in any form, by any means, now known or yet to be invented, including mechanical, electronic, photocopying, recording, videotaping, or otherwise, without the prior written permission of the publisher. No one shall upload this title, or part of this title, to any social media websites.

The right of Brian Clemens to be identified as author of this work has been asserted by him in accordance with Section 77 of the Copyright, Designs and Patents Act 1988

SHOCK!

Presented at the Palace Theatre, Westcliff-on-Sea, on the 30th April 1974, with the following cast of characters:

Ann Marsh	Ann Kennedy
Jenny Rayner	Lesley Grayburn
Terry Dexter	Simon Brent
Andy Flewin	Michael Graves
Steve Turner	David Becket
Peter Rayner	Philip Brack
Maggie Miller	Jenny Tarren

The play directed by Leslie Lawton

Setting by Dorothy Draper

The action takes place in Maggie Miller's country home, a converted windmill

ACT I Friday afternoon
ACT II Immediately afterwards
ACT III
    Scene 1 Saturday afternoon
    Scene 2 Two hours later
    Scene 3 Monday morning

Time—the present

ACT I*

The interior of a large windmill, now converted into a house

Early afternoon

The conversion has been a thoughtful one, retaining much of the original character: an area of architectural interest and surprise. To one side and to the front of the stage is what might be loosely termed the "relaxing" area; here are some comfortable chairs, an occasional table, and a battered chesterfield. Beyond them a door leads off to a box-room. On the opposite side is an openwork wooden staircase leading up a few feet or so to where a kind of balcony/gallery runs along the wall. Off this gallery are two doors leading to bedrooms. Situated half-way along the gallery is a large oak coffer—open—its lid up. Close by the bottom of the stairs is a very, very small dining table and chairs. On the table is a telephone. Also, nearby, is a small statuette, a figurine we will see more prominently later. At the top of the stairs hangs a small Chinese wind chime hung at such a level that one might or might not accidentally brush against it while passing and set it tinkling distinctively. Between these two areas we have a virtually unobstructed view to the back of the stage—where, just off centre, is the main door leading directly in from outside. Above the door is a fairly deep transom window. To one side of this door, opposite from the stairs, almost facing us, is a tall cupboard with two long doors. To the other side is a modern kitchen unit, adjoined by a complex of modern kitchen cupboards. Just above the sink unit is a large window to the outside—an original window, set higher than one would normally set a "kitchen" window—so that, although one gets the impression of trees and space beyond, one does not get an eye-level view out. If anyone were standing outside it, one would be looking just over the top of their head. Near the sink unit is a rack containing bric-à-brac and a long kitchen knife. On a table is hi-fi equipment—also a tape-recorder. This is set prominently

One feels that this is the "main" area of the conversion—the place where one cooks, drinks, entertains, relaxes—the place where everything happens

The conversion is the home of Maggie Miller, a young air-hostess and, through the furnishings and bric-à-brac we should come to know her very well. She travels—there are many objets d'art *from many countries—including a Samurai sword wedged against a beam. She has a sense of humour—some of the bric-à-brac is frankly bawdy—bought for their amusement value. She is a modern young woman—mingled with the antique bric-à-brac are modern "Op" art items, and a great deal of the kitchen stuff is brightly coloured. She has style; the whole area evokes this*

---

*N.B. Paragraph 3 on page ii of this Acting Edition regarding photocopying and video-recording should be carefully read.

When the CURTAIN *rises, the sun is shining outside: as the Act proceeds the outside light fades slowly, almost imperceptibly, until by the end of the Act it has changed from day to dusk, and the whole area is very shadowy. The whole area seems utterly empty for some moments—then we hear movement from the shadowy gallery—and suddenly the lid of the open coffer is closed. A man, Peter Rayner, is revealed standing there. He is about thirty, handsome, with a face full of character, a face not to be forgotten easily. He wears well-cut country clothes we will remember, and when he moves, he moves lightly, like an athlete. He remains by the coffer for a moment, tapping his fingers on the lid as though to say, "That's that!" There is something altogether furtive and guilty about his manner, about his presence here. We feel he does not belong here. Now he reacts as he hears the sound of a taxi approaching some way off. He is galvanised into action—he hurries down the stairs to the main door. Here he stops, rather urgently feels in his pocket for something. Finally he produces a fairly large door-key. He tosses it in his palm—then quickly opens the main door and exits. The door closes behind him—we hear the door being locked and then we see his hand appear through the transom to replace the key. Then the hand disappears*

The sound of the taxi is very loud now. It stops and becomes the familiar tick-over sound of a taxi. We hear a taxi door open and shut

Taxi Driver (*off*) Can I give you a hand with that, miss?
Ann (*off*) No, thanks, I can manage.

We hear the taxi start up and pull away again—and, as the sound recedes—we hear a knock at the door—then another

Maggie? Maggie?

The sound of the taxi has gone

We see Ann's hand appear at the transom window—take down the key there—we hear the door being unlocked—then the hand replaces the key again—and then the door opens and Ann Marsh enters. She might be anything from thirty-five to forty-five—a trim, very attractive woman who wears the figure-flattering uniform of an airline. She looks exactly like a stewardess, but actually she is part of ground operations. Despite her obviously groomed assurance there is a sense of fun about her; we like her immediately. She carries a smart week-end case, and a wrapped parcel or an anonymous bag large enough to contain a dress

Ann Maggie. Maggie? (*She does not really expect an answer, and is not at all alarmed—she knows her way around this place; she is at home here. She pauses to touch a certain item*) Oh, you're new. (*She sees a large chunk of card prominently propped up against the tape-recorder, with some message printed on it. She picks it up and reads*) "Darling. Have just popped into the village to pick up the cake. Make yourself at home." All right, I will. (*She puts down her case—determines that the kettle is filled—plugs it in—then takes the teapot lid off and picks up a large tin marked "Tea". It is empty. She goes to the tall cupboard, opens the right-*

Act I

hand door and reveals shelves of foodstuffs. She starts to rummage for fresh tea)

We see Jenny's hand appear at the transom, feel for and find the key—then the door opens and Jenny Rayner enters. Jenny is an attractive woman of about thirty

The open cupboard door screens Ann from Jenny, and vice-versa. For a few moments neither is aware of the other—as Jenny closes the door, then heads straight for the record-player—seems about to operate it—and then is startled as Ann closes the cupboard door

Hello. (*She blithely moves back to charge the teapot with tea*) Sorry if I startled you. I was just making some tea—join me?
Jenny Thanks. (*Amused*) Do you usually offer tea to strangers?
Ann You're no stranger. You're Jenny Rayner, aren't you?
Jenny Why, yes.
Ann Maggie's told me all about you.
Jenny I didn't expect to find anyone home. When the key's there—it usually means Maggie's out.
Ann (*her tea-making preparations completed*) I put it back, force of habit. And she is. Maggie. She is out. Popped into the village. (*She picks up her case and heads for the stairs*) I'll just put my things away, watch the kettle, will you? (*She starts to ascend the stairs*)
Jenny You must be Ann Marsh.

Ann stops and reacts

Ann Oh, I'm sorry, I . . .
Jenny Don't worry, Maggie's told me all about you, too.

Ann ascends the stairs and exits into the first bedroom door off the gallery

Jenny remains gazing after her for a moment—then suddenly she turns about and starts quickly to search the place—finally finding an ashtray—and taking from it a longish cigarette-end. She holds it up, stares at it, then turns to move and regard the tape-recorder again—her hands touch it

Ann enters from the bedroom with a parcel

Jenny hastily, guiltily thrusts the cigarette-end down behind a chair cushion, or similar place of concealment, and turns to face Ann

You must wonder what I'm doing here. I came to borrow a book, that's all. I often do that, take a walk through the woods, let myself in and . . .

Ann is preoccupied, moving to open the parcel or bag and to take out a distinctive party dress, to shake out the creases and hold it on its hanger

Ann (*interjecting*) Maggie's always kept an open house. I sometimes think *too* open. (*She turns quickly to Jenny*) Oh, I don't mean you. But living in such a lonely place as this—the key so obvious—anyone could get in. You're her nearest neighbour, aren't you?
Jenny Yes, we live about a mile away—beyond the wood. Peter and me. Peter's my husband.

Ann Yes, she's told me about him, too.
Jenny Oh, really?

Jenny might pursue this line of conversation but at this moment Ann shakes the dress free and holds it up to examine it

Ann It's travelled better than I thought, won't need to iron it after all.
Jenny For the party?
Ann Yes.
Jenny It's beautiful.
Ann You think so?
Jenny Mmm, I just wish *I* could afford something like it . . .
Ann Afford? How much do you think it cost then?
Jenny I know how much it cost. I saw this self-same dress in Harringhams just the other . . .
Ann (*interjecting*) Harringhams? (*She flourishes the dress—and then hangs it somewhere in the area*) Fifteen quid from the little *boutique* on the corner!
Jenny No!
Ann Afraid so. (*She moves to finish making the tea*) I know I shouldn't admit it, but, well—Maggie's spoken of you so often, I feel I'm just confiding in an old friend.
Jenny Yes, I feel the same about you. (*She produces cigarettes*) Cigarette?
Ann No thanks, I don't smoke.
Jenny Like Maggie. She doesn't smoke either.

Ann hands Jenny tea

Thanks.

A pause, they sip their tea

Ann Perhaps it's not so bad for Maggie, I mean she's away so often—hardly ever here—but you—don't you find it lonely living here?
Jenny I find it—restful. And anyway, the country is such a marvellous place to bring up the children.
Ann Oh, Maggie didn't tell me you had children.
Jenny Well, we don't. Not yet. But sooner or later . . . Children are the final expression of love, aren't they?
Ann So they say.
Jenny What did Maggie tell you about Peter?
Ann Eh?
Jenny You said she told you about Peter, what did she say?
Ann Well, that he's your husband, a promising architect, good neighbour —attractive . . .
Jenny She told you that?
Ann Why? Isn't it true?
Jenny (*smiling*) Yes, of course. At least, I think so.
Ann And so does Maggie.
Jenny Yes. (*She turns her attention to the hanging dress*) I was planning to wear just jeans or something, but if you're going to be wearing *this* . . .
Ann Maggie said "casual" and these days that can mean anything from a

T-shirt to a tiara. I just felt like dressing up because—well—I just felt like it, that's all . . . (*After a slight hesitation*) Your husband is about the same age as you, isn't he?
Jenny Two years older. Why?
Ann Just curious. (*Slight pause*) No. Can you keep a secret?
Jenny Probably.
Ann Tonight could be a double celebration—Maggie's birthday—and my engagement!
Jenny That's wonderful!
Ann That's why I bought the dress—but you mustn't breathe a word, not until it's official. All these years with the airline—chasing a career . . . Oh, there have been men, of course, but never *one* man. *The* man . . .
Jenny Until now.
Ann Yes. I love him, Jenny. I love him so much.
Jenny And he loves you.
Ann I think so.
Jenny Well then . . .
Ann But he's younger than me. Nearly five years younger.
Jenny Well, that's hardly a generation gap. More of a generation crack!
Ann You really think it doesn't make any difference?
Jenny Why should it? If you love each other . . .!
Ann Yes. (*Smiling*) I had to tell *someone*.
Jenny I'm glad you did. And I'm happy for you. But, Ann, don't be taken in. Make sure. Quite sure!
Ann What?

Jenny abruptly moves away to the bookshelves

Jenny (*examining and discarding books*) Pay no attention to me. This is my day for cynicism.

Ann, a bit uncertain, moves closer

Ann That's not bad—if you like frothy romance.
Jenny Mmm. I expect she keeps the best books locked away somewhere.
Ann Best books?
Jenny How long have you known Maggie?
Ann Since I helped to train her—how to soothe the savage passenger and not spill soup into his ear—that kind of thing.
Jenny But you don't know about the books.
Ann Books? What books?
Jenny The spicy, kinky books. The porny ones.
Ann (*laughing*) What?
Jenny Maggie brings them back from abroad. Smuggles them in.
Ann (*still amused*) She told you that?
Jenny No. She showed me. I was telling her about—about a friend of mine whose husband isn't being as attentive as he was—and Maggie produced *her* method, as she called it.
Ann A pornographic book?
Jenny Yes.

Ann One book doesn't make a collection.
Jenny It isn't just books.
Ann What do you mean?
Jenny I'm sorry. Maggie's a friend of yours and I shouldn't be . . . Look, let's forget the whole thing, shall we?
Ann Oh, no, I want to know what you meant by that last remark. "Not just books." What did you mean?

Jenny regards her and hesitates

Jenny All right. It's this. (*She moves to touch the tape-recorder*)
Ann The tape-recorder?
Jenny I don't think she meant to tell me—but she'd been drinking and it just slipped out.
Ann What did?
Jenny If men were butterflies, Maggie would pin them to a card, but they're not—so she does the next best thing. The next worst thing. She puts them on tape.
Ann (*laughing*) One, two, three, testing . . . !
Jenny (*interjecting*) No! No, Ann. Not talking. Not *just* talking. Every gasp, every murmur—every . . . You know.
Ann I don't believe it. Whenever Maggie has an affair—whenever she makes love . . . ?
Jenny She commits it to tape.
Ann I do not believe it. This recorder . . . ? (*As she speaks, she presses the button*)
Jenny No!

Jenny is too late—the tape turns—and, from the recorder comes the sound of pleasant music. It plays for a few moments—and then Ann snaps off the recorder again and turns to look sympathetically at Jenny

Ann You don't like Maggie much, do you?
Jenny Yes, yes, I do like her. I *do*. But . . .
Ann (*quietly*) But?
Jenny I always feel so *plain* when she's around.
Ann But, Jenny, you're not a bit plain.
Jenny Dull then. When she starts talking about all the wonderful places she flies to—places I'm only ever likely to *read* about—it sounds so—so glamorous. So exciting.
Ann Excitement—glamour? Yes, it's sometimes like that I suppose. But not always . . .

Jenny regards her with some compassion

Jenny I'd forgotten. You were in a bad air crash, weren't you? Maggie told me. A bad air crash and you were the only survivor?
Ann (*with bitter-sweet irony*) Yes, I was the lucky one.
Jenny It must have been awful—a terrifying experience.
Ann Mercifully I don't remember. I was in a coma for weeks—and the rest—I've taught myself to forget.

Jenny That must be strange—in a coma, life ticking away and you're there, not knowing—strange—and yet—comforting.
Ann Comforting?
Jenny There are times when it might be nice *not* to know what's going on around you. (*More forthright*) It helped you blot out the crash, didn't it?
Ann Perhaps. (*More sharply*) Anyway, since then I've had both feet firmly on the ground.

Ann reacts to the sound of a sports car approaching, horn blowing a tattoo, skidding to a stop outside

That's Terry! (*Moving to open the door*) Terry Dexter—Maggie's latest!

Terry Dexter enters. He is a handsome man of about forty—an airline captain, dressed at this time in casual clothes. He carries some birthday parcels

Terry Ann. (*He grips Ann, kisses her, bends her right back as though they are doing a tango and eventually rights her and acknowledges Jenny with the explanation*) We're quite good friends. Dexter. Terry Dexter—and you must be . . . (*to Ann, frowning*) Who must she be?
Ann (*laughing*) Jenny Rayner.
Terry (*shaking hands*) Jenny. Heard about you. How do you do? Don't answer that in case it gets me too excited and blots my copy book!
Ann Te-rry! It's good news then?
Terry The very best. Arteries all pounding away quite normally—and my heart's in the right place.
Ann (*affectionately*) I always knew that. Congratulations, Terry.
Terry Thanks. (*Very sincerely*) And I mean it. A very nasty moment.

Ann embraces him—then becomes aware of Jenny who is watching him askance

Ann Sorry. You must think we're both mad.
Terry Not both. Just you—*I* clearly have all my marbles. Isn't that right, Jenny?
Ann Terry flies for his living.
Terry Only thing I know how to do well—we-ll, barring one other activity I can't possibly discuss in front of ladies.
Ann He flunked his last medical.
Terry Just the merest semiquaver on the old blood pressure . . .!
Ann Nevertheless, they grounded him—but now you're O.K. again. Right?
Terry Right! It was simple really. I just laid off the booze and the centre pages of *Playboy* for a while—and yesterday I coughed twice and nothing rapidly descended—so they gave me my licence back! (*Seriously*) Which is a real relief, Ann. One semiquaver . . .
Ann Have you told Maggie yet?
Terry No, I tried to call her, but I couldn't get through.
Jenny The line's probably down. Ours is. It's the wind.
Ann Well, why didn't you leap into your car and come charging over?
Terry Only thing that charges in *that* heap is the battery—and not even

that yesterday. The bloody car wouldn't even whimper, let alone start. Still, this is better, isn't it? A big birthday surprise for Maggie . . . Where the hell *is* Maggie anyway?

Ann Gone into the village to pick up the cake.

Terry Oh? Many people coming to this party?

Ann I don't know. You, me—Steve—Jenny here—her husband . . .

Jenny Oh, yes, Peter will be here. Definitely.

Terry That's five slices of cake already.

Ann Yes.

Terry And knowing Maggie's leaning towards excess—it's bound to be a big one—so I'd better give her a hand, don't you think . . . ?

Ann We-ll . . .

Terry Don't want her having a hernia, do we? Not just when *I've* been passed fighting fit. (*He opens the door*) I'll go and meet her.

Ann She's probably half way home by now.

Terry Then I'll meet her half way. I've had plenty of practice at that.

Terry exits—during the following we hear his car start up and move away

Jenny (*after a slight pause*) So he's Maggie's latest acquisition. Is it serious?

Ann With Maggie? Your guess is as good as mine. I hope so though. I've known Terry for years, he's—he's O.K.

Jenny How do you know Maggie's gone to the village? Was she here when you arrived?

Ann No, she left this note—see?

Ann hands Jenny the chunk of card—Jenny scans it

Jenny So there was nobody here when you arrived—nobody at all?

Ann No. Why?

Jenny meanders away

Jenny Me—Peter. You—*Steve* . . . ?

Ann *My* latest acquisition. Steve Turner—you wouldn't have met him, but he's just about the . . .

Jenny (*interjecting*) Oh, but I have.

Ann What? But how? *Where* did you meet him?

Jenny Right here. Last Thursday, I think. Yes, last Thursday. I dropped by and he was here, having coffee with Maggie.

Ann Here?

Jenny Steve Turner. She introduced us. He was sitting right there. By the tape-recorder.

Ann That's very odd. Steve knows Maggie of course, he's met her a couple of times—but—why didn't he tell me he'd been down here?

Jenny He probably forgot. Or—he didn't want to worry you.

Ann reacts, stares at her

Well—Maggie's reputation as a man-eater . . .

Ann A part of you hopes that's true, doesn't it?

Act I

Jenny reacts

Steve—my Steve—and Maggie having an affair, that would take a load off *your* mind wouldn't it, Jenny?
Jenny I don't know what you mean!
Ann Yes, you do. "What did Maggie say about Peter?" "Who was here when I arrived?" You expected to find your husband here, didn't you?
Jenny No!
Ann You half suspect he's having an affair with Maggie.
Jenny No! No! (*Suddenly putting her hands to her face*) Yes. Oh, I don't know, Ann. He's fascinated by her. He never stops talking about her. Sometimes I think, if he mentions her name just once more, I'll—(*her hand makes a fist as though clutching a knife*)—I'll . . . (*She waits*) I don't know.
Ann Well, I do. Maggie's many things, but she's not a home-breaker. (*More brightly she picks up the tea and biscuits she has taken from the cupboard, opens the right-hand door and starts to replace them*) At forty thousand feet they say a man feels nearer his God—but he *certainly* feels farther from his wife—and the number of married men who've had the "no" sign from Maggie, are . . . (*She stops dead as she reacts to the interior of the cupboard*) That's odd.
Jenny What is?
Ann (*producing a cake festooned with candles*) Maggie's birthday cake!

Jenny reacts and picks up the card

Jenny "Darling. Have just popped into the village to pick up the cake . . ."
Ann (*putting the cake on the table*) She must have been up and out early this morning. (*With a sudden thought*) But where is she now? Gone back to the village to pick up more booze?
Jenny No, that was delivered yesterday. (*She opens the cupboard wider to reveal stacked bottles on the lower shelf*) Two crates of bubbly—see? No! She's somewhere else. With Peter!
Ann Jenny . . . !
Jenny It's possible, isn't it? It's possible . . . ?
Ann (*over-riding her*) Jenny, there could be a hundred and one last minute things she had to attend to.
Jenny No, she's with Peter—with my husband . . .
Ann Jenny . . .
Jenny Or your precious Steve!

Ann regards her for a moment, then turns away

Ann You're being very foolish.
Jenny And cruel. I'm sorry, Ann . . .
Ann Let's forget the whole thing and have a drink, shall we? I mean, it's about time for a drink, isn't it?

Jenny nods—Ann moves to pour two drinks, adding tonic water from the refrigerator

Jenny I really am sorry. I shouldn't have said that. I—what I mean is—I like you, Ann. Talking to you—it helps.

Ann hands Jenny a drink

I want to have a baby!

Ann Sorry, I can't help you with that one! Have you thought of mentioning it to your husband?

Jenny He used to be all for the idea. Until we moved here—met Maggie . . .

Ann Hey, hey. We were going to forget that—remember?

They toast and drink—Ann eyes Jenny

You've plenty of time. You're still young. (*She drains her glass*) If you *are* so worried about Peter and Maggie why not clear the air? Ask him direct—see what *he* has to say . . .

Jenny Oh, I couldn't, I just couldn't . . .

At this moment the door opens and Andy Flewin enters. Andy is dressed fairly rough—one might take him for a handy-man, an odd-jobber, save that he is a little young for the work—about twenty-six—and as we shall see, a little too intelligent. He is not a Cockney, but not public school either. His voice has the rough and readiness we have come to describe as "classless". Under his arm he carries a large, flat parcel, wrapped in brown paper. He breezes in quite informally—and then stops as he sees Jenny and Ann

Andy Oh, hello. Magg . . . Miss Miller not home then?

Ann Not yet, no.

Andy Right.

Andy puts down the parcel—then moves across the area and goes into the box-room

Ann turns questioningly to Jenny—Jenny gestures—she has no idea who he is: so Ann feels impelled to go to the box-room door

Ann Excuse me . . . ?

Andy puts his head around the door

Andy Has she moved it, then?

Ann What?

Andy Little tool box she usually keeps in here. Hammer and nails—haven't seen it, have you?

Ann No, but I . . .

Andy I'll have another look then.

Andy exits into the box-room again

Ann turns to gaze helplessly at Jenny

(*off*) Ah, yes.

Andy enters from the box-room, carrying a small tool box. He moves across, then begins to study a wall area at the back of the room

Act I

Not symmetrical. Never looks right if they're too symmetrical. Yes. (*Some kind of decision made, he now pulls round a chair with a soft cushioned seat—and proceeds to stand on it—and then begins to mark a spot on the wall—marking it hugely with a big black pencil—and then he begins to drive a nail into the wall*)

Jenny and Ann can only stand and stare askance as Maggie's room is raped in this way

Ann This may sound like a silly question—but just who are you?
Andy Doesn't sound silly at all. Not the way you say it. (*He carries on hammering in the nail, then pauses, regards it, and speaks over his shoulder*) Flewin. Andrew Flewin. Andy to my intimates. (*He steps off the chair and regards the nail*) Lovely. (*He blithely moves past Ann to pick up the parcel*) 'Spect you're wondering what I'm doing?
Ann Frankly—yes.
Andy Thought you were. I can tell. (*He climbs on to the chair again, holding the parcel*) I'm the hangman, aren't I? Here to hang Maggie Miller. But don't worry, I'll make a pretty job of it. Painless, too. She won't feel a thing.

As Andy talks, he rips off the brown paper to reveal a framed canvas—its back to us. As he proceeds to hang the painting, Jenny and Ann obviously realize his reason for being here

Ann I see.
Andy No, you don't. Not yet. (*Then with a little air of ceremony, he fixes cord to nail—and steps back and we see clearly for the first time, that the painting is a large nude study of Maggie Miller*)
Jenny It's Maggie!
Andy For her birthday. In her birthday suit.

Jenny and Ann stare at it for a long moment—moving closer to it. Meanwhile, Andy helps himself to a drink

Ann Who painted it?
Andy I never sign 'em. Not the nudes. That way, you don't get trouble with husbands later.

Jenny and Ann turn to stare at him as he blithely drinks Maggie's drink

Ann You?
Andy I. With my little palette. (*He moves up to regard the painting*) Not bad is it? If I hadn't known the subject I would have called it, "Virgin Waiting Hopefully For Her Prince to Come".
Jenny I've never seen you before.
Andy Before what? Before Christ? Before the pound was devalued?
Jenny Where are you from?
Andy Twelve Station Road, Ormskirk.
Jenny I mean around here—where's your studio?
Andy (*grinning*) My studio? That way—down towards the river.
Jenny There's nothing there—except a ramshackle old farm . . .

Andy My studio.

Jenny I've heard about you. A tramp, a layabout hippy living rough . . .

Andy (*for the first time seriously—almost snarling*) I'd say I was living free! Rough by your silly bloody middle-class standards, perhaps, but as far as I'm concerned . . .

Ann (*interjecting*) There's no need to be so bloody rude!

Andy stops, regards her, then grins

Andy You're right. Got nothing against you. Nothing. Apologies are in order, ladies.

Jenny You've only been in the district a month at most.

Andy Yes, a bit too soon to run for councillor, don't you think?

Jenny And yet you've got to know Maggie . . .

Andy (*over-riding her*) She's easy to know, that one.

Ann moves to stare at the painting

Ann A month. And in that time, you've met her—she's posed—you've painted.

Andy I'm a fast worker.

Ann regards him—and at this moment we hear Terry's car speeding back to a stop

Ann How about boy-friends?

Andy What?

Ann You don't sign the nudes because of trouble with husbands. How about boy-friends?

Before Andy can answer, the door opens and Terry enters

Terry The oddest thing, I went to the cake shop and . . . (*He stops as he sees Andy*) Oh. Oh, I don't think we've . . .

Andy Andy Flewin.

Terry Dexter—Terry . . .

Ann Mr Flewin is a painter.

Terry Eh?

Ann draws his attention to the nude—Terry stares at it

Good God!

Andy Good it is. God it ain't. She meant it to be a surprise—Miss Miller—a surprise, she said. I have a distinct feeling she achieved it. Right. Well then—I'll be back later.

Ann Will you?

Andy She hasn't paid me yet. And I like to be paid. (*He opens the door, then pauses*) Funny you didn't say.

Terry Say what?

Andy Whether it's an exact likeness or not. Being her boy-friend and that, I'd expect you to make an informed assessment. Cheerio.

Andy exits

Act I

Terry stares after him, then at the painting

Terry What the devil is Maggie playing at!?
Ann You didn't find her then?
Terry Find her? Of course I didn't find her! I don't know what this is all about, but the chap in that bloody cake shop insisted—(*He stops as he sees the cake on the table—stares at it*)—and he was right!
Ann Terry, what are you talking about?
Terry This cake. Maggie collected it *yesterday* morning!
Ann Yesterday?
Terry Yesterday. *That* was the day before today.

During this, Jenny again picks up the card and studies it

Jenny Then who was this note intended for?
Terry Eh? (*He takes the card, scans it, frowns at Ann, then tosses the card down again*) It's another of those silly bloody jokes of hers. Has to be . . .
Jenny Jokes?
Terry Maggie's warped sense of humour. Like in San Remo. (*To Ann*) You remember San Remo? (*To Jenny*) Maggie pretended she was drowning—and got four life guards plunging in to save her. Big, bronzed; with muscular jock-straps!
Ann (*in a strange, strained tone*) This isn't like that.
Terry Oh, I dunno, change of venue perhaps but . . .
Ann (*interjecting*) *This isn't like that!*

They regard her

How long since anyone saw or spoke to Maggie?
Terry Eh? Well, the chap at the cake shop told me that she popped by yesterday and . . .
Ann (*interjecting*) It's more than twenty-four hours.
Terry (*puzzled*) Well?
Ann There's something wrong.
Terry How do you mean?
Ann Maggie invites us down here to celebrate her birthday and she's not here to meet us—and there's a cake already collected, and a note more than a day old—don't you find that all strange?
Terry Strange?
Ann *Disturbing.*
Terry Bloody rude if you ask me—it's usual to ply one's guests with intoxicating liquors—which reminds me . . . (*He picks up the bottle and pours a stiff one*)

Ann and Jenny regard him—he becomes aware of it

Now what's wrong?
Ann (*gently*) That semiquaver in blood pressure.
Terry Hah! (*He drinks a swig, and regards them defiantly*) I passed didn't I? Good for another six months? (*Defensively*) Anyway, perhaps I *need* a drink, did you consider that? Perhaps Captain Terry Dexter *needs* to imbibe!

Jenny Why?
Terry That's my business.
Jenny What have you found out? It's Peter isn't it?!
Terry Who the hell is Peter?
Ann Jenny's husband.
Terry Peter. Paul. Tom-Dick-Harry—she wouldn't tell me his name.
Jenny But there *is* somebody else?
Ann (*calmly over-riding her*) What *did* Maggie tell you?
Terry She's "found a new play-thing". Those were *her* words. "A new play-thing." (*He drains his glass*) Wanted me to give her time. To find herself. To sort herself out. Well, I sorted her out all right. "A new play-thing." (*He swings round to stare at the painting*) That painter feller, d'you think?
Ann He's only been around a few weeks—she could hardly know him . . .
Terry Well enough to bare her boobs at though. To give him the full frontal. *And he certainly knows her.* (*He continues staring at the painting*)
Jenny Oh God, it's Peter. I know it's Peter.
Ann Terry, when did Maggie tell you?
Terry Does it matter *when*? She told me. That's enough.
Ann Yet you still came down this week-end.
Terry (*with an ironic grin*) You're looking at the Prototype World's Number One Stupid Bastard. Yes, I still came down because I—well, because I still . . . (*Forthrightly*) Because I fancied a week-end in the country! (*He turns and stares out of the window for a moment or two. Then he abruptly turns—he is his "old self" again*) And it's going to be fun. I promised myself, and I promised Maggie it would be fun.
Ann *When* we find Maggie.
Terry Oh, come on—that's square one. You—are spreading alarm and despondency—and why? For what reasons? What do you think's happened to Maggie, eh? (*He grabs up the Samurai sword, and jerks it from its sheath*) Think she's been swagged away by the Seven Samurai? Ha—so!

Ann and Jenny stare at him—he reacts, relaxes a bit

Ann Terry, the sword!
Terry Huh?
Ann Look at the sword. It's covered in blood!

Terry reacts—stares at the sword, touches the tacky blood stain

Terry Jesus!
Ann It *is* blood.
Terry I dunno—might be. (*He puts the sword down, with the first sign of a growing alarm*) Where else might Maggie be? Well—she isn't here—she has to be somewhere! Where?!
Jenny Betty Canvey's place—she may have gone there to borrow some records.
Terry Right. Do you know the number . . . ? (*He picks up the telephone—*

Act I

then instantly drops it back again) Forgot, it's not working. Where does this—Betty Canvey live?
Jenny Storpington. The big white house on the corner.
Terry Is Betty Canvey young and pretty?
Jenny No, about fifty, very plain.
Terry I won't be long then.

Terry opens the door, but Ann moves to him

Ann Terry—the police, don't you think we should . . .
Terry I don't think we should panic or do anything silly—not until we've checked everything first.
Ann But, Terry . . .
Terry (*firmly over-riding her*) No point in arousing the whole country—and then have Maggie walk in—she wouldn't thank us for it. I'll take the back road—be as quick as I can.

Terry exits

We hear the sports car receding, then Ann turns to regard the sword

Jenny He shouldn't have taken the back road.
Ann Eh?
Jenny This time of the year it's like a quagmire. He may not get through.
Ann It *is* the quickest way.
Jenny Not if you get stuck.

Each is just talking to conceal her real feelings

Ann Something's happened to Maggie.
Jenny We don't know that.
Ann *I* do.

Jenny regards her

Jenny I need another drink.

Jenny up-ends the liquor into her glass, then finds the tonic-water bottle empty—and moves to open the refrigerator, remains there, then laughs lightly. Ann reacts

Ann What is it?
Jenny Don't you see? Barbecue steaks—for tonight's party. All neatly cut up—with *that*.

Jenny indicates the sword—Ann regards it

Ann It's—it's possible I suppose.
Jenny Last year she carved the Christmas turkey with it. (*She drinks*) Mystery solved. (*The mood leaves her*) A part of it anyway. (*She turns away*) It *is* Peter, I know it is! (*She turns to Ann*) Look at the facts.
Ann What facts?
Jenny You heard Terry—"She's found a new play-thing". *A new plaything.* Peter.

Ann You don't know that. "Someone new"—it could be the butcher, the baker—(*with a sudden thought, as she whirls to regard the painting*)—the painter...

Both regard the painting—then we hear the sound of the sports car zooming back to stop at the house. They both react—Ann hurries to the door

Terry! (*She opens the door*)

Terry enters

What's happened?
Terry I couldn't get through on the back road.
Jenny I told you...
Terry Maggie's car is blocking the road!
Ann What!
Terry Stuck in the mud about half way up.
Ann And Maggie?
Terry No sign of her.
Ann But where would Maggie have been heading?
Terry Where you said, I suppose. To see this Canvey woman. Could she walk it from there?
Jenny It's possible, but...
Terry Right, then.
Ann But if it's only half-way up the back road, why wouldn't she have come back here? It doesn't make sense.
Terry Find that out when I find her! I'll have to take the long way round to Storpington now. (*He opens the door. Ruefully*) Some birthday.

Terry exits

Ann slowly closes the door behind him—Jenny watching her—and we hear the sports car start up and recede

Jenny Storpington's more than two miles. (*With a sudden thought*) My place would be nearer. Much nearer. *Our* place.
Ann If Maggie had gone to your place you would have seen her on your way here.
Jenny I didn't take the back road. It's quicker through the woods. Unless you're driving. If you were driving, you'd take the back road—stop about half way—then walk through the edge of the woods to my place. Then...
Ann Jenny! You're just guessing again.
Jenny No, no, no...
Ann *Yes.*
Jenny She's there now, in my house—with Peter. Peter and Maggie, they're together and... (*She suddenly moves away—then stops, and turns to regard Ann*) I must find out if they *are* there together. You understand that?
Ann Yes, I understand.

Jenny opens the door

Act I

But, Jenny . . .

Jenny pauses

I'm sure you're wrong.
Jenny I hope so. Dear God I do hope so. But if I am—where does that leave you? And Steve?

Jenny exits

Only after the door has closed does Ann give way to emotional stress—she sags, looks around the area

Ann Oh, Maggie—Maggie—where are you? (*Suddenly she feels the need to disperse the gloom of the atmosphere. She rises from the chair, moves to snap on the tape-recorder. Bright music—continuing from when and where we last heard it—begins to play. She gathers up the cups and glasses and starts to wash them up*)

A pause. Ann works busily—and then, from the tape-recorder we hear an unmistakable laugh—a woman's laugh, deep, throaty, wicked. Ann reacts. She spins round towards the tape-recorder. The music plays on—but mingled with it we now hear sighs, whispering—the sound of two people making love. Ann, despite herself, is impelled to move back towards the tape-recorder. The love-making sound continues with music in the background. Suddenly voices are heard on the tape

Maggie's Voice What's wrong with you today? The radio bothering you, is that it?

There is a sharp click—the music stops—there is a silence, broken only by the whisper of clothes

I thought you liked music while you work. (*She laughs*) While you're on the job.

We hear the sound of someone standing up, moving away

Steve's Voice Come on, let's go upstairs.

Ann's hands fly to her mouth

Ann Steve! (*She reacts to what follows*)
Maggie's Voice I like it down here.
Steve's Voice It feels too damned public.
Maggie's Voice Whatever you say, Steve, my darling . . .

We hear sounds of movement—then the sound of Chinese chimes—then Maggie's laughter

Steve's Voice Now what?
Maggie's Voice I was just thinking—if Ann could see us now!
Steve's Voice Don't even joke about it. As it is, I don't know how I'm going to face her at your party tomorrow. I'm going to have to tell her about us, you know.
Maggie's Voice Don't be a bloody fool! What the eye doesn't see . . .

Steve's Voice I'll have to.
Maggie's Voice Oh, no you won't. I won't let you—I'll see to that.

There is the noise of a door slamming. Then silence—the tape-recorder runs on. Ann remains, a broken figure, staring at the recorder.

> *Behind Ann, we see the second bedroom door slowly opening. A figure, Steve Turner, enters—but is too dark and shadowy to discern shape or sex. We are merely aware of a figure gently moving along the gallery towards the head of the stairs—almost at the stairs, it touches against the Chinese chime and sets it tinkling*

Ann freezes to the sound—then forces herself to turn—sees the figure at the head of the stairs

Ann (*scared—tentatively*) Maggie . . . ?

The figure continues down the stairs. There is no hint of stumbling or swaying, rather a slow, deliberate movement. The figure reaches the bottom of the stairs—then slowly advances towards a transfixed Ann—and, when the figure moves into the spare light near Ann, we at last see that it is a man of about thirty-five to thirty-eight—a handsome man—he wears pyjamas or a robe, and has been hacked to pieces with a Samurai sword—his clothes and body are saturated with blood. He stands regarding Ann—and then thrusts a bloody claw towards her

Man (*in a whisper*) Help me.

He falls at her feet. Something snaps inside Ann, and she begins to scream three terrible screams, as—
the CURTAIN *falls*

ACT II

The same. No time has elapsed

As the CURTAIN *starts to rise we hear again Ann's three terrible screams. She is standing staring down at the bloody figure of the man, who lies on the floor. His wounds are made more horrible by virtue of the fact that he wears only pyjamas, and the back of his jacket is torn to ribbons*

Ann Steve! (*She crouches beside him—to lift and cradle him despite the blood*) Steve—Steve.

We now realize that the man is Steve Turner, Ann's boy-friend. Ann holds him close

The door is suddenly slammed open, and Jenny enters, turning on the lights

Jenny Ann? I heard you screaming half a mile away and . . . (*She stops as she sees Steve. She moves further into the area—regards Steve for a long moment—then abruptly she turns to the sink. We hear her making retching sounds, see her shoulders heaving. Finally, she controls herself then turns, forces herself to move back towards Ann and Steve*) Where!

Ann Upstairs. He must have been upstairs the whole time. He was up there the whole time!

Steve moans softly and moves ever so slightly

Ann We must get a doctor!

Jenny What happened? Has he said anything? Has he said what happened?

Steve moans again—then arches up—extends a hand towards Jenny—then his hand stiffens, and he falls back—still—dead

Ann For pity's sake—he needs a doctor!

For a moment Jenny does not move—then she bends beside Steve and examines him briefly

Jenny No. Not any more.

Ann holds Steve closer, staring at Jenny

He's dead.

Ann stares at her a moment longer

Ann (*holding Steve close*) No—no—no! Steve—Steve—my darling . . .

Ann crouches close over Steve in her anguish, and begins to cry. Jenny can only stand by and watch. There is a long pause until Ann's crying subsides, and she can finally bring herself to lift her head and regard Jenny helplessly. Ann gets to her feet and moves towards the sofa. Jenny would intercept, but

Ann shrugs her aside and, with a kind of terrible lucidity overcoming her, she takes the dress from where it hangs and moves to cover Steve with it

Suddenly, startlingly, there is a knock at the door. Ann and Jenny swing round towards it—then they hear a scraping sound—then the sound of the key going into the lock—then the unmistakable creaking sound that the front door makes as it is opened. But the front door remains shut! Only then do Jenny and Ann swing round towards the tape-recorder—which is still running—realizing that what they hear emanates from there. They hear the front door closing. Someone moving around—then the sound of a bedroom door opening. They turn towards the gallery—almost as though they are seeing the tableau they are hearing

Steve's Voice You're imagining it.

Maggie's Voice No, I'm sure I heard someone downstairs. I'd better take a look.

We hear Maggie's footsteps along the gallery—then the tinkle of the Chinese chimes—then footsteps descending the stairs

(*After a pause*) Darling! This *is* a surprise. I—I'd given you up for lost. I expected you early this morning. You see, I even left a note for you.

We hear a rustle of paper

Then—when you didn't turn up I—made other arrangements.

Steve's Voice Maggie—come back to bed!

A long silence

Maggie's Voice Darling—please. No! No!

We then hear a distinctive metallic sound—then a crash—as though the tape-recorder has been knocked over. Then—silence again. A long pause as Jenny and Ann stare at the tape-recorder—stunned by its revelations. Eventually Jenny speaks

Jenny That last sound—sharp—metallic . . .

In answer, Ann picks up the Samurai and draws it from its sheath. The sound it makes is that heard last on the tape-recorder. They regard one another grimly—then Ann puts the sword down and moves to the tape-recorder—starts to run it on fast

Ann There might be more.

But the tape-recorder plays on in silence. Ann is about to give up, then she hears a definite sound on the tape—unidentifiable because she is running through fast. She instantly presses the normal play button—and, from the tape-recorder we hear the faint sound of someone whistling—whistling tunelessly—the sound rising and fading as though the someone were moving around the room. It continues for some moments—then silence. Ann snaps off the tape-recorder

Run out. (*She turns to regard Jenny, then moves to look at Steve's body*) One of us has to fetch the police.

Act II

Jenny Yes.
Ann I'll stay with him. But what about Maggie? We still haven't found Maggie! (*She turns to look up at the gallery*)
Jenny Oh God, you don't think . . .?
Ann *Steve* was up there.

Ann moves to stand by the stairs, looking up at the gallery. Tentatively, she mounts a stair, then looks back at Jenny

Jenny I can't! So help me, I couldn't bear to go up there!

Ann regards her a moment longer, then turns and ascends the stairs alone. Jenny watches as Ann moves along the gallery

Ann exits through the second bedroom door

Instantly, Jenny rummages down a chair cushion to retrieve the cigarette-end she put there earlier. She hurries over to the sink, drops the cigarette-end into it, turns the tap and flushes it away. Then she hurries to the Samurai sword and rubs the handle free of fingerprints with the skirt of her dress

Ann enters from the second bedroom as Jenny completes wiping the sword

Jenny turns to stare up at Ann, who remains immobile for a moment, then finally shakes her head

Ann Nothing.

Ann descends the stairs—and we see from her bearing that she has now recovered from her hysteria—she is calm and efficient again. She steps off the stairs

You'd better go and get the police.
Jenny Yes. (*She moves to the door, then stops and turns*) But not yet, Ann. We'll call the police—but not now. Not right away!
Ann But, Jenny . . .
Jenny (*interjecting*) Let me find Peter first—let me talk to him!
Ann Peter?
Jenny I haven't seen him all day. *I haven't seen him since yesterday afternoon!*

This statement hangs on the air for a moment. Ann stares at Jenny, who moves towards her

I just don't know where he is!
Ann A little while ago you thought he was at your house—with Maggie!
Jenny I was just fooling myself. Even the thought of him being there with Maggie was better than not knowing. (*She paces away, trying to assemble her muddled thoughts*) I went into the village yesterday. Peter was at home when I left. But he was edgy, restless—as though he had something on his mind. When I got back—he'd gone. So I came over here.
Ann Here!
Jenny Yes. The house was dark. I knocked and I knocked, but I couldn't make anyone hear—and then—I suddenly got an uncanny feeling that

there *was* somebody here. I listened at the door and I—I thought I could hear someone breathing, just the other side of the door . . .
Ann (*sharply*) So then you let yourself in?
Jenny No. I couldn't. The key wasn't there. That's why I'm *sure* there *was* somebody here.
Ann (*grimly*) There was.

Jenny reacts

Steve.

Jenny turns to stare at Steve's body

Jenny No, it wasn't him. I *know* it wasn't him. Somebody else—whoever . . . (*Suddenly*) Please, Ann—let's not call the police yet!
Ann But this was murder!
Jenny I just want a chance to talk to Peter first.

A pause. Ann considers, then finally nods

Ann All right.
Jenny Oh, thank you, thank you.

Ann turns to stare at Steve's body

Ann But I can't bear to look at him like that—to see him—like that . . . (*She turns to regard Jenny*) We'll have to move him.

Jenny reacts

Jenny I—I can't. I couldn't bring myself to touch him . . .
Ann (*interjecting*) I'm giving you time, Jenny.

Ann moves away to open the box-room door, then she moves back to Steve's head. She turns to regard Jenny. Jenny remains a moment, then fearfully moves to Steve's feet. They lift Steve with difficulty, and move to the box-room door

Jenny and Ann exit to the box-room, with Steve's body, returning after a moment having left it there

Jenny, trembling, moves to a chair and sits. Ann, maintaining an ice-cold calm, closes the box-room door. She moves to regard Jenny—then wordlessly pours a large drink and pushes it into Jenny's hand. Jenny drinks deeply, recovers a little, and looks up at Ann

Jenny What about you?
Ann (*dully*) What about me? "Lesson One: don't panic—don't—*show* your panic. It's infectious. The passengers look at you." So keep smiling, pouring the drinks—keep calm—even though you felt the lurch—know what it means. Even though you can see the flames licking around the port engine—keep—smiling . . . (*She ends with a choking cry and buries her face in her hands*)

Jenny regards her—realizing just how very close she is to breaking. She

Act II

quickly gets to her feet, pours a drink and hands it to Ann. Ann merely raises her head and stares at her

Jenny The shock's just starting to hit you. *Drink it!*

Ann drinks it down. Jenny would recharge the glass but Ann gestures her aside

Ann No, no—I'm all right now. Thank you, Jenny. (*She paces away*) Where will you look?

Jenny Look?

Ann For Peter. That's why you want time, isn't it? To find Peter?

Jenny Yes.

Ann But there's more to it than that, isn't there, Jenny? More than you've told me?

Jenny No. Yes. That is—I don't know—I'm not sure.

Jenny moves back to the tape-recorder, snaps it on and runs it backwards. We hear the whistling—fast—backwards. Then Jenny snaps the tape-recorder—pushes the button—sets it running forwards—normally. Again the sound of tuneless whistling fills the room. Then, as suddenly, she snaps it off

(*with a nervous laugh*) Whoever it is—he can't hold a tune.

Ann Jenny, what is it?

Jenny snaps on the tape-recorder again. Again tuneless whistling fills the room

Jenny!

Jenny It's always been a joke between Peter and me . . . (*She stops dead*)

Outside we hear someone whistling tunelessly. Jenny snaps off the tape-recorder—the recorded whistling stops. But the whistling outside continues—tuneless whistling—like that we have already heard. Ann and Jenny turn to the door—riveted for a moment—and then we see—a hand reach up to the transom—feel for and find the key—and then disappear again. Ann reacts—she pulls Jenny back into concealment as we hear the door being unlocked—then the hand is seen through the transom replacing the key

The door creaks gently open and Peter Rayner enters. He is the man we saw at the very beginning of the play

Peter gently closes the door behind him—then, his movements cat-like and furtive, he quickly moves across the area to the stairs. He ascends the stairs, moves to the coffer on the gallery, opens it—and then Jenny steps out of concealment

Jenny Peter!

Peter is so surprised that he drops the coffer lid down again with a bang, and spins round to look down at Jenny and Ann. He is utterly taken aback—and then confused

Peter J—Jenny. Darling. I—I didn't think—I didn't expect to find you . . . (*He blurts out*) Where's Maggie?

Ann *That*'s what we want to know!

Peter Sorry, I don't follow . . .

Ann (*over-riding him*) Where is she? What have you done to her?
Peter What the devil . . . ? (*He starts to descend the stairs*) Who is this?
Jenny Ann Marsh—a friend of Maggie's.
Ann (*interjecting*) Where *is* Maggie?
Peter I DON'T BLOODY WELL KNOW! Perhaps you don't remember —but it's the first question *I* asked.
Jenny (*over-riding him*) What are you doing here, Peter? And where have you been since yesterday?
Peter I'll tell you. (*Regarding Ann*) But later. In private. This is something between just you and me . . .
Ann Oh, no. You'll tell us now!
Peter Look, I'm rapidly losing patience with you . . .
Jenny She has a right to hear what you have to say.
Peter Right? *Right!* Why? Am I allowed to ask that?
Ann Because you whistle out of tune, Mr Rayner!
Peter (*staring at her*) What!?
Jenny Tell us where you've been! (*In anguish*) Please, Peter—*just tell us that! Please!*

Peter stares at Jenny, astonished and concerned by her anguish, yet still not fully understanding it

Peter I went walking—will that do?
Ann No!
Peter You keep out of this!
Jenny Peter, it concerns her—it concerns all of us!
Peter What does?
Ann You—Maggie . . .
Peter Will you keep quiet! (*To Jenny*) Jenny, what is it? What's going on here?
Ann Let's have your explanations first . . .
Peter (*rounding on her*) Now look here—I told you to keep out of . . .
Ann (*interjecting*) No—you look here! (*She jerks open the box-room door*) Here!

Jenny reacts, and takes a hesitant step forward

Jenny No . . .
Ann (*firmly over-riding her*) It's the only way we'll convince him, Jenny. Here, Mr Rayner!

Peter is slightly taken aback. He hesitates and looks at Jenny, who steps back, nods, then turns away. Peter regards her, then again looks at Ann by the door

Peter (*finally, with a shrug*) If only to humour you . . . (*He strolls across to the box-room door and starts to exit through it*) Though *what* I'm supposed to be looking at . . .

Peter exits into the box-room—there is a profound pause and a silence— and then suddenly he dashes out again, totally shocked

Act II

Jesus Christ! Jesus Christ! (*He can find no other words for the moment. He stares back at the door again. Sotto voce*) Jesus Christ! (*He turns to stare at Ann and Jenny*) Who is he?
Ann (*emotionally*) His name was Steve. Steve Turner. Are you beginning to understand now?
Peter (*stunned*) Understand . . . ?
Jenny He was here yesterday with Maggie.
Ann And now Maggie is missing.

Peter seems to be having trouble fitting the facts together

Peter Maggie . . . ? (*Rounding on the box-room door*) But who *did* that—who?
Ann That's what we are trying to find out, Mr Rayner.
Peter You don't think that I . . . ? (*Swinging round to Jenny*) *You* don't think that, darling—you can't . . . !
Jenny No, of course not. (*To Ann, defensively*) You saw him—he was as shocked as we were . . .
Ann He could be faking.
Jenny No! (*To Peter*) You must tell us where you've been!
Peter (*still very confused*) I told you—walking . . .
Ann You'll have to do better than that. Walking where—and why did you come here just now—and what's upstairs—in that coffer?
Peter Coffer?
Ann Maggie is still missing.
Jenny Oh God—no, Ann—it can't be . . .
Ann He came in here and went straight to it. It's big enough. Wide enough. What's in it, Mr Rayner?

Peter regards them, then he picks up the drink bottle, puts it to his lips and swigs from it for a moment. Ann pulls it from his mouth

You want me to go up there and see for myself!?

Jenny reacts. Peter turns and moves to mount the stairs

Peter You want to know what's in the coffer? You really want to know? Then I'll show you—I'll show you! (*He moves along the gallery to the coffer, slams back the lid, stares into the coffer for a few moments—then plunges his hands into the coffer and produces a woman's head! For a moment or two it looks like a real one—then we see it is a painted, ceramic head, intended as an ornament. He comes down the stairs holding it. Bitterly*) Maggie's present! My special birthday gift to her! With a suitable inscription of course. (*He fumbles for a card attached to the head, and reads*) "For dear sweet Maggie—from Peter!" (*Suddenly his mood turns to resignation*) That's the stinking pity of it all! (*He turns to Jenny*) That you had to find out *now*.
Jenny I already knew.
Peter No. You suspected maybe, but you didn't *know*. You need never have known.
Jenny I was bound to find out sooner or later.

Peter If it had gone on—yes. But that's the whole point, darling. I'd made up my mind to finish it. It *is* finished! That's why I came here—to get this—(*he flourishes the head*)—to take it away, and forget about Maggie once and for all!

Jenny stares at him, not sure whether to believe him or not

Jenny (*murmuring*) Oh, Peter . . .
Ann Very glib.

Jenny and Peter part, and turn to look at Ann

He still hasn't told us where he's been for the past twenty-four hours—or explained the whistling.
Peter Whistling? What is all this about whistling?
Ann You were whistling when you came in here . . .
Peter Certainly. I often do. (*Grinning*) Jenny will tell you. Always whistling . . .

As Peter talks, Ann moves to the tape-recorder and manipulates it

Ann This was recorded *after* Steve was killed.

She snaps it on—and again we hear the tuneless whistling. Peter listens for a moment

Peter That's right. That's me!

Ann reacts, snaps off the tape-recorder, and turns to regard Peter. He is very matter-of-fact, as he takes out a cigarette and lights it

I can explain. (*Sadly, regarding Jenny*) But, darling, I wish . . . (*Sharper*) Oh, hell! (*He puffs his cigarette alight*) Yesterday I couldn't get Maggie out of my mind. I *knew* she was just playing me along. I had to see her. I came over here about six-thirty. There was nobody home—so I let myself in, and sat down and waited; and I drank a little too. (*Ironically*) And then I drank a lot. And I waited. But no Maggie. I stayed here all night, but she didn't show up . . .
Ann (*interjecting*) All night?
Peter Yes. Right through until today . . .
Ann But Jenny came here last night.

Peter reacts, and turns to look at Jenny

Peter Jenny?

Jenny hesitates

Jenny It must have been some time after nine . . .
Ann (*interjecting*) She came here and knocked—she knocked several times.

A pause. Peter regards Jenny for a long moment

Peter I must have dozed off. I got stinking drunk and fell into a stupor.

Act II

When I woke up it was today. Well into today. Oh—one-thirty maybe. I heard someone coming—a taxi . . .
Ann (*interjecting*) That must have been me.
Peter Maybe. Anyway, I stashed Maggie's present away, and got the hell out of here!

A slight pause

Ann And what have you been doing since then?
Peter I told you—walking.
Jenny Oh God, I didn't have to do it!
Ann (*reacting*) Do what?

Jenny turns to face Ann, and hesitates

Jenny (*who could be lying*) Cover up for Peter.
Peter What do you mean?
Jenny I wiped the handle of the sword clean—I got rid of a cigarette-end I thought was yours . . .
Peter But why on earth did you do that?
Jenny Don't you see—*then* I thought it might have been *you* who . . .
Ann (*coldly interjecting*) And it still might be! Only *one* person can give us the absolute truth . . .

Peter and Jenny look at her

Maggie. When we find her.

A slight pause. Ann moves to look at the sword, then, more decisively, she turns

We've wasted enough time. We have to call the police now.
Peter (*to Ann*) Well, go ahead, then—call them, why don't you?
Jenny The phone isn't working.
Peter Oh! (*Moving towards the door*) I'd better start walking then . . .
Ann (*over-riding him*) No!

Peter stops and regards Ann

Jenny can go.
Peter But it's a hell of a way to the nearest . . .
Ann (*interjecting*) Jenny can go. And you stay here, Mr Rayner.
Peter I *see*. Afraid I won't come back?

Ann merely looks at him. He gestures

Jenny Peter, I'll go—I don't mind going . . .

They all freeze, as we hear Terry's sports car speed up and stop. The horn pumps out a gay tattoo. Footsteps approach. Ann and Peter step apart

The door opens and Terry enters. He is alone, and grinning cheerfully

Terry Well, we can all stop worrying, old dears!
Ann You've found Maggie?
Terry No, but I know where she is. Hello, you must be Peter. Dexter—

Terry Dexter. (*He moves to pick up the bottle and starts pouring a drink*)
Ann Well, where? Where is she?
Terry Gone to town.
Jenny Town?
Ann How do you know?
Terry Superior intelligence—the grey matter—that what lifts us above the apes . . .
Ann Terry!
Terry I had a brain-wave and had a word with the local cab service. One of 'em remembers picking Maggie up here at about six o'clock last night—and taking her to the station! So that's it then—spur-of-the-moment trip to town—we all know Maggie's liable to do things like that. Her car breaks down—she abandons it—summons a local carriage —simple explanation. (*He turns to survey the grim faces of Peter, Jenny and Ann*) Well, what's up with you lot! You look as though you were at a funeral!

A slight pause

Peter I'm very much afraid that we are.
Terry Eh?

He looks around. They regard him

Come on, what's the joke?
Jenny It's Steve Turner.
Terry Steve? Yes, a bit late getting here, isn't he? Still, never very punctual our Steve. That's what they'll put on his headstone—"The Late Steve Turner"!
Jenny Terry—Steve is dead.
Terry What? Oh my God, Ann—I'm sorry—I didn't know . . . (*He moves to Ann, but she turns away*) How did it happen? An accident?
Peter He was murdered.
Terry Murdered! What do you mean—murdered? (*His attitude is still one of only half-belief*)
Jenny Killed. In this house. His body is in that room.

Terry stares from the door of the box-room to the faces of the others

Terry You mean it, don't you? You really mean it?

No-one moves

> *Terry regards them a moment longer, then slowly moves to open the box-room door. He gazes in for a moment, reacts, then slowly exits into the box-room*

A slight pause

> *We hear Terry's muffled curse, and he enters from the box-room, very shaken*

Terry He's been hacked to pieces. (*More sharply*) What about Maggie?

Act II

Jenny No sign of her.
Terry (*pacing away*) Then she did go to town. (*He turns*) Who found him?
Ann I did.

Ann turns away. Terry regards her compassionately

Terry (*softly*) Dear God . . . (*More forthright, he indicates the box-room*) But not in there? With those wounds he'd have bled like a pig and there's no . . .
Ann (*interjecting*) He was killed in Maggie's room. It's like a—a slaughterhouse up there.
Terry In Maggie's room?
Ann Yes.
Terry And he's wearing pyjamas.
Ann Yes, yes!

Terry regards her, then paces away

Terry I still can't believe it—who would want to murder Steve?
Ann You!

Terry spins round to face her

Or any one of us here.
Terry ⎫ Why the hell would I . . . ⎫ (*Speaking*
Peter ⎭ Good God, I didn't even know the man . . . ⎭ *together*)
Ann (*cutting across them both*) Listen . . .! LISTEN! (*She moves to the tape-recorder, pushes the button to wind it back, stops the tape, then pushes the button to press it forward at normal speed*)

The voices are heard. Terry and the others listen, riveted

Maggie's Voice Darling! This *is* a surprise. I—I'd given you up for lost. I expected you early this morning. You see, I even left a note for you. Then—when you didn't turn up—I—made other arrangements.
Steve's Voice Maggie—come back to bed!
Maggie's Voice Darling, please . . . No! No!

Again we hear the sound of the Samurai sword being drawn—again the crash —and then silence. Ann snaps off the tape-recorder and turns to regard the others

Terry (*tautly*) What else is on that tape?
Ann Nothing that adds anything. Just Steve's last words. And perhaps Maggie's, too.
Peter You're talking as though you *knew* she was dead!
Ann Isn't she? What does this tape mean? The sound of that sword leaving its scabbard—a crash—and then—nothing. Well, if she isn't dead—where is she?
Terry I dunno any more.
Peter "Darling." Obviously someone she knew well.
Terry She calls everyone "darling".
Ann Including you, Terry.

Terry What are you driving at?
Ann The facts.
Terry What facts?
Ann That any one of us might have killed Steve.

Terry makes a disgusted, scoffing noise and turns away

All right, let's start with you. You get through your medical—your first instinct is to tell Maggie. But *you* say the phone isn't working . . .
Terry Well it isn't, dammit!
Ann It isn't *now*. I shouldn't think it's too difficult to disable a phone. So what next—your car? But that wasn't working either . . .
Terry Nor was it—I told you . . .
Ann (*interjecting*) Which garage repaired it, Terry? We can always check.

Terry hesitates, then speaks grudgingly

Terry I fixed it myself. But I bloody well promise you I . . .
Ann (*interjecting*) So it is possible you were lying. It is possible you *did* come down here yesterday—you found Maggie with another man . . .
Terry (*interjecting*) But I already told you I *knew* there was someone else . . .
Ann Oh, yes—you *told* us. After the event.

Terry stares at her—then gestures and turns away

Terry All right—so I'm Suspect Number One.
Ann No just—suspect. *I'm* Suspect Number One.

They all react, and regard her

Steve meant more to me than any of you. To find him in bed with Maggie . . . Yes, I think I could have done it. I *could* have done it . . . (*Sharper*) But so could Peter Rayner! (*She advances on Peter*) It was a good story—very convincing. But, it could be just a story.

For a moment Peter regards Ann, then he shrugs

Peter What's my motive?
Ann The same as Terry's. Another man.
Peter But I told you . . . (*He stops, gestures wryly*) I forgot—just *telling* you isn't enough. O.K. I accept what you say—I'm just as good a suspect as you or Terry—but what about Jenny? You said all of us—but what possible motive could *she* have for killing Steve?

Ann turns to regard Jenny

Ann Because she thought it was you!
Peter What! Oh, come on . . .
Ann (*interjecting*) Why not? The curtains are drawn up there—the room's dark—and Jenny's been conditioning herself for days that she was going to find you in bed with Maggie!
Peter But Steve called out—you heard him yourself . . .
Ann A vague voice, coming from upstairs—saying the one thing she

Act II

dreaded to hear: "Come back to bed, Maggie"? She might easily have thought it was you.

Ann and Peter regard Jenny. A pause, then Peter steps towards Jenny

Peter Well, Jenny . . . ?

Jenny does not answer

Say something!

Jenny What is there *to* say? I suppose what she says could be true . . .

Terry (*wryly*) We'll never know what's true until we find Maggie. For God's sake—where is Maggie!

The telephone suddenly rings—it is the first time we heave heard it, and the effect is shattering and shocking. Terry, Peter, Ann and Jenny all turn to stare at the telephone—all fearful of answering it. It rings and rings for some moments, then Jenny, who is nearest, takes a tentative step, stretches out her hand, touches the telephone and finally picks it up

Jenny (*into the telephone*) Hello? . . . Oh, yes, I see. Thank you. (*She replaces the receiver—turns to the others*) The operator, to say the line is working again!

Terry looks at Ann

Terry You see—I *told* you it was out of order.

Determinedly Ann strides over to pick up the telephone—and begins to dial. The others watch her. She finishes dialling. A slight pause

Ann (*into the telephone*) Police!

Terry reacts and takes a step forward, but Peter stops him

Peter No, she's right. We've dabbled around long enough.

A slight pause

Ann (*into the telephone*) Police? My name is Ann Marsh. I want to report a murder . . . Yes, a murder! . . . The Old Mill, Amerhill . . . Yes . . . Thank you. (*She hangs up and turns to face the others*) There's a car in the area—should be here soon.

Terry What a mess!

Terry moves to stand leaning over the tape-recorder for a moment, then turns away and starts to help himself to a drink. There is a pause—each of the group is now occupied with thoughts of what lies ahead. Peter seems to be very calm—he leans against the stairs

Peter Maggie left here in a cab yesterday evening?

Terry realizes Peter is talking to him; he turns, drink in hand

Terry That's right. (*At Ann*) Mind you—you only have *my* word for it.
Peter Did the driver know Maggie?
Terry Er? I dunno . . .

Peter How did he know it was Maggie then?
Terry *Because I described her.* What are you driving at?

Peter turns to regard Ann

Peter The suspects. You made one important omission.

Ann stares at him

Maggie herself.
Terry *Maggie?*
Peter What does a murderer usually do? *Run from the scene of the crime.*
Terry He's right—he's absolutely right. But what about motive?
Peter I don't know—Maggie's life is such a mix-up. Anyway, there might be a dozen reasons why she'd want to kill Steve . . .
Ann (*over-riding*) She couldn't have done. Unless . . .
Terry Unless? Well, come on, Ann—unless what?
Ann He—Steve said to Maggie that he was going to tell me the truth about what was going on between them . . .
Terry "Steve said to Maggie . . .?" (*Realizing*) You said there was nothing else on that tape!
Ann I said there was nothing that added anything. Nothing that concerned you—or any of you—just—me and Steve!
Peter How did Maggie take that—when Steve said he was going to tell you . . . ?
Terry Let's hear for ourselves.

Terry moves to the tape-recorder, but Ann bars the way

Ann No!

Terry stops, then capitulates

Maggie got angry. She—she said she wouldn't let him do it.
Peter There you are then. Perfect motive.
Jenny Of course—it *was* Maggie who killed Steve!
Ann It might have been. Just as it might have been one of us.
Peter But the fact remains—*we* are all here—and Maggie isn't. (*He moves over to look at the Samurai sword*) Could a woman have used this with such force?
Terry If she were aroused. *Angry* enough. And I've seen Maggie angry. By God, I've seen her! (*For a moment he is lost in thought—then is more forthright*) Let's leave it to the boys in blue, eh? They'll be here soon enough. Meanwhile—why don't we all have another drink?

A slight pause

Peter (*to Jenny*) I think you ought to. It isn't going to be pleasant.
Terry No, sir! (*As he talks, he opens the right-hand door of the cupboard, takes down some glasses, closes the door again, sets out glasses, and begins to pour drinks for all of them*) The way they probe and ferret and try to trip you up. Two of 'em usually—snapping questions at you until you're so punchy you'll admit to anything . . .

Act II

Ann You seem to know a lot about it, Terry.

Terry freezes, his back to her, then he turns, glasses in hand

First-hand knowledge?

Terry regards her for a moment, then laughs shortly and hands Ann her drink

Terry Had a little run-in with them once.
Ann When?
Terry Few months ago.
Ann I never heard about it.
Terry It didn't get into the papers, if that's what you mean. Why should it? Just a bit of a barney in a pub.

Terry buries himself in a drink, Ann still bears in on him

Ann A barney?
Terry (*irritably*) A fight then!

Terry paces away. The others watch him. After a slight pause he rounds on them

(*Defensively*) I took exception to a bloke—said so—he said something back—so I hit him. End of story. Satisfied? (*He paces away, growing more restless every minute*)
Ann I didn't know you could be so violent.
Terry Perhaps there's a lot of things you don't know. (*Thoughtfully*) And some things *I* don't know. This tape-recorder for instance. How come it was recording anyway?

A pause. Ann and Jenny exchange a look

Jenny One of Maggie's perverted little pleasures. Everything on tape.
Terry Everything?
Jenny But *everything*.

Terry stares at the recorder

Terry My God—I'm immortal! You play this right through?
Ann Well—no. I think there were a few feet at the front—but just music.
Terry *Music.* (*He sets the tape-recorder rewinding*) Let's see, shall we?

As the tape rewinds, Peter moves to pour himself a drink. Then he moves nearer to the tape-recorder: Ann too, Jenny remains where she is

Ann Terry, I don't think you should listen to this . . .
Terry That's the one thing I'm going to do!

He snaps on the tape-recorder—it starts to play. For a moment there is silence, then music breaks in. This plays for a few moments, then we hear love-making sounds. This continues for a few moments

Maggie's Voice (*whispering*) Steve . . .

We hear love-making sounds. And then—back to square one—we hear Maggie's throaty wicked laugh again.

Ann (*breaking*) That's enough! (*She snaps off the tape-recorder, turns away and murmurs*) Enough.

There is a silence—but the memory of the tape-recorder hangs over them all

Terry The newspapers are going to have a field day.
Peter I never knew about that side of Maggie. We ought to wipe that tape.
Terry Just what I was thinking...
Jenny (*to Peter*) Why are you so worried? You swore that nothing ever happened between you...
Peter Terry's right—can you imagine what the papers will make of this?
Terry Exactly. We should wipe this tape—find the others and destroy them...
Ann No! I won't let you do that.
Terry But, Ann...
Ann *A man has been murdered*. And somewhere on that tape there may be a clue to who did it. I won't let you do it!
Terry Ann...

Terry takes a step towards her, but gets no further because there is a knock at the door. They all freeze and turn towards the door

Jenny The police...
Terry It can't be—didn't hear a car.

There is another knock at the door—and finally Terry opens it

Andy enters

Andy Hello, again. She back, then?
Terry Who? Oh, you mean Maggie.
Andy That's right. Obviously not, or she'd be rushing at me by now—plying me with words of an admiring nature—a few five pound notes—and— (*noting the drinks*)—perhaps a glass of Scotch. It's a thirsty day—my throat's dry as a temperance hotel.
Terry (*amiably*) Like a drink, would you?
Andy You must be psychic.
Ann Terry...
Terry (*with a warning look*) Have a drink by all means. As a matter of fact, we are expecting more company any minute—company I feel you ought to stay and meet.

Ann and the others get the message

Andy (*his glass charged, he moves away, close to Peter*) Hello—get over your problem?
Peter (*startled*) Eh?
Andy Oh, you don't know me—but I've seen you. Yesterday, as a matter of fact—lurking about the area. There, I thought, is a man with a problem.

A small pause. Terry moves forward to recharge Andy's glass again

Act II

Terry Obviously you notice things going on around you.
Andy Part painter's eye. Part plain nosey parker.
Ann And what were you doing around here yesterday?
Andy Didn't say I was around here. Did I?
Peter You saw me.
Andy Ah, but I didn't say WHERE I saw you, did I? (*He drinks*) Will she be long?
Terry Maggie? No, no—just nipped out—er—but I forgot—she left a message for you!

The others are intrigued, not knowing where Terry is leading

Andy Oh?
Terry Yes, it's the painting ...
Andy Don't she like it?
Terry Oh, no, she likes it fine—but you've hung it in the wrong place ...
Andy She distinctly said ...
Terry (*over-riding him*) She actually wanted it in her bedroom. Over the bed.
Andy Over the bed?
Terry Yes, there's a hook there—just waiting.

A pause

Andy Well, I hate to keep a hook waiting. Better oblige I suppose. (*He moves to reach up, unhook the painting, and then move with it towards the stairs*) Be sort of poetic. A nude over the bed—and one in it.

Andy ascends the stairs—all eyes on him as he moves along the gallery. He reaches the second bedroom door, then senses something, stops dead, then turns

Which door?
Terry The one you're standing right in front of!
Andy Ah!

Andy exits into the second bedroom

Ann moves to Terry

Ann Terry, what do you think you're doing ...?
Terry (*softly*) Give him enough rope—he might just hang himself ...
Ann I don't understand.
Terry Didn't you say it was like a slaughter-house up there?
Andy (*off*) Here!

Andy enters from the second bedroom in a rush, still clutching the painting

Have you seen up here?
Terry Something wrong, Mr Flewin?
Andy Wrong! There's blood everywhere—bed, ceiling, walls, everywhere ... (*He stops as he surveys their faces—all tilted to look at him*) But you knew didn't you? You sent me up here and you knew ... (*He starts to descend the stairs*) What's your bloody game, then?

Terry half turns away to pour himself another drink—he up-ends the bottle over the glass—it is empty. He goes to the cupboard, opens the right-hand door and takes out a fresh bottle of Scotch

Terry Oh, I'll grant you it's bloody—but not a game, Mr Flewin.
Andy I don't know what you're talking about—but up in that bedroom there's . . .
Terry (*interjecting*) You'll know—as soon as the police get here.
Andy (*faltering*) Police?
Terry They'll be here any minute—and they're going to be asking you *plenty* of questions—about you—and Maggie . . .

As Terry talks, Andy reacts. He puts the painting down near the foot of the stairs, then lightly vaults the last couple of stairs and runs towards the door. Terry moves to intercept him

Where d'you think you're going?
Andy Police are bad news where I'm concerned—they'll move in and say *I* did it.
Ann Did what?
Andy Don't worry, they'll think of something . . .

Andy lunges for the door and gets it half open. Terry grapples with him—but Andy is very strong

Terry No, you don't. Help me . . .

Peter rushes in to help, he grabs Andy, too. All three struggle and, locked together, bang against the big cupboard then sway out across the room again.

Andy Let go of me, you bastard . . .!

During this part of the struggle—the left-hand door of the cupboard slowly starts to swing open for the first time. Andy punches Terry, knocks him down and away to the ground, and is just tackling Peter when the cupboard door opens fully. We see that on this side of the cupboard there are no shelves, just a long, shallow space—and wedged into this space is the body of Maggie Miller! Her blood-caked hair has fallen forward to partially screen her face—so one does not need an exact match to the portrait. Blood stains her body and the torn nightdress she wears. Peter and Andy struggle. Terry is on his feet, just moving in to assist, when Ann sees the body. She half cries out, drops her glass. Everyone freezes now—all turn towards the cupboard to stare at the body. At this instant one of Maggie's arms flops out to hang lax, stained with blood

Ann *Maggie!*

Curtain

ACT III

Scene 1

Late afternoon the next day

The set is empty, but there is plenty of evidence of a vigorous police search—both cupboard doors are open and we see that Maggie's body has gone. The box-room door, indeed the door to every cupboard or closet in the area is open. Furniture has been moved around, ornaments have been moved around. The Samurai sword has gone; the tape-recorder, too. The painting leans—propped near the foot of the stairs

Ann enters from the first bedroom door. She descends to the main area below—there is an air of resignation or weariness about her. She stops at the foot of the stairs, surveys the area with a sigh, then starts to move to tidy the place up a bit. She starts to close all the doors—when she gets to the box-room door she hesitates for a moment, remembering Steve—but closes the door with an air of finality, and moves to the tall cupboard. Again there is a slight hesitation, but this time she quickly overcomes it, closes both the doors, turns her back on the cupboard and moves to tidy up around the area. As she does this she sees, and reacts to a medium-sized, rather distinctive figurine that has been in the set the whole time, but now, owing to the police upheaval, has been brought to a place of prominence. Ann looks at the figurine—moves on, then stops, returns to pick up the figurine and turn it over in her hands, thoughtfully examining it. We hear the sound of Terry's car approaching, stopping, footsteps coming to the door. Ann reacts, puts the figurine down again, temporarily forgetting about it as she turns to the door

The door opens and Terry and Jenny enter—Jenny very distraught, Terry half supporting her. Jenny wears a distinctive coat

Ann What's happened?

Terry lifts a warning finger—then helps Jenny to a chair, and sits her down

Where's Peter?
Jenny The police are holding him.
Ann What!
Terry For "further questioning". They're holding on to Flewin too . . .
Ann (*compassionately*) Oh, Jenny . . .
Terry Don't worry—Peter'll be all right, you see. It's that bloody Flewin character they ought to concentrate on. (*He sees that he is getting in the way of Ann comforting Jenny*)

Jenny Peter just shrank away. I—I—never saw that happen to anyone before. When they started questioning him—I saw it happen. He went white—began to shake, and something left him—spirit, courage, I don't know what you'd call it—just left him. Then—he turned to me and said . . . (*She starts to cry—unable to continue*)
Ann Jenny . . .
Jenny (*blurting out*) He said, "*Oh God, Jenny, they really think it was me!*"

Jenny breaks up again—unable to continue. Terry and Ann look at each other

Terry They'll see their mistake soon enough, once they wade in on Flewin . . .
Jenny (*crying*) And it's all my doing—*my* fault!
Ann (*with an edge to her voice*) Why, Jenny? Why is it *your* fault?

Jenny remains with her head in her hands for a moment or two, then finally she lifts her head again—she seems more in control of herself

Jenny (*hesitatingly*) Because . . . (*More forthrightly*) Because I made him admit he was here all last night.
Ann We both did that.
Jenny All right—*our* fault then! If *we* hadn't made him do that, he need never have said he was here at all!
Terry (*toughening up*) You're forgetting one thing . . .

Jenny looks at him

He just *might* be guilty.
Ann No.
Terry What?
Ann I don't think Peter did it.
Terry Now just a moment—not so long ago it was *you* who made out a pretty solid case against him!
Ann I thought he *might* have done it *then*. But I don't any more.
Jenny What changed your mind?

Ann moves to pick up the figurine

Ann This did.

Jenny and Terry exchange a look, then Terry takes the figurine from Ann, examines it, and looks at her questioningly. Ann takes it back from him

Just over a week ago Maggie and I were in town. And *this*—(*the figurine*) —was in Harringham's shop window.

A slight pause. Ann puts the figurine back on the table and regards it

Maggie took a fancy to it. (*She turns to face Jenny and Terry*) Maggie said she intended badgering someone into buying it for her—for her birthday. I think Maggie succeeded. I think someone *did* buy it for her.
Terry (*after a pause*) I don't see where this is leading.
Jenny (*very tensely*) I do. We *know* what Peter bought for her.

Act III, Scene 1

Jenny picks up the ceramic head

This. We were here when he came to retrieve it . . .

Ann touches the figurine

Ann So who gave her this? Who did she "badger", Terry?

Terry What the hell does it matter?

Ann Oh, but it does matter. It matters very much. Don't you see—this didn't just suddenly appear—it's been here the whole time. I've been aware of it, but I just didn't connect it before.

Terry Connect it with what!?

Ann With Maggie's murder! (*She picks up the figurine again*) It's been here *the whole time*—so whoever gave it to her must have brought it along *before any of us arrived yesterday!*

Jenny (*in a low monotone*) And whoever brought it—murdered Maggie.

Ann It's possible.

Terry (*sarcastically*) Possible? Anything's possible. It's possible it was *posted* here, did you consider that?

Ann regards the fragile figurine

Ann Something as fragile as this? (*She shakes her head*) I doubt it.

Terry O.K. So it's a nice, new, wild theory—but it lets *me* out!

Ann and Jenny stare at Terry. He gestures

Well, you were both here—you saw me arrive with *my* packages—*my* presents for Maggie! Well, look—look!

Terry moves to where his packages still remain. He holds them out to Ann and Jenny

You see?

Ann regards him, then turns away

Ann You had plenty of time to plan things—to see this loophole and cover it up.

Terry Good God! What do I have to do to satisfy you! And come to that —what about *you*? (*To Jenny*) And you! What did you get for Maggie, eh? What presents did you buy for her?

Ann I bought her mine when we were in town last week—a nightdress. She was—(*falteringly*)—she was wearing it . . .

Terry regards her with some sympathy

Terry All right, so that's *you* clear. (*He turns on Jenny*) Now it's *your* turn.

Jenny does not answer. Ann turns to regard her

Jenny I—didn't get her anything yet. I—I wasn't sure. I meant to ask her what she wanted . . .

Terry We-ll. Maybe you did just that, eh? Maybe you *did* ask her—and she said, "Well—there's a very nice figurine in Harringham's window..."

Jenny (*interjecting*) No! I never heard her mention it. I promise you.

Terry stares at her

Terry I suppose your word is as good as mine. (*To Ann*) Or yours—or anybody's . . .! (*He turns away, then stops, reacts and begins to laugh*) And there's someone else to consider!

Ann There isn't anyone else!

Terry (*grimly*) There was. *Steve.*

Ann (*reacting*) Steve?

Terry Maybe *he* bought it for her. Or maybe Maggie bought it for herself. Of maybe it just isn't bloody well important! I don't know any more. All I do know is that Peter's stuck in a cell, and I feel sorry for him. Don't ask me if he's guilty or not guilty—I just feel sorry for him. If there was something I could do—*something!* (*He is wound up for a moment. Then he turns with a change of manner, and takes the figurine from Ann*) It's out of our hands now. Come on, forget it and . . .

Terry makes to put the figurine back on table. He fumbles with the figurine—drops it or "accidentally" knocks it against the table—either way, it is smashed—the pieces fall to the floor. A shocked pause. Ann stares at Terry. He regards her, then steps back a pace or two

It was an accident. *An accident!* (*He turns to where Jenny is staring at him*) Well, don't look at me like that! (*Suddenly he clenches his fist—and is momentarily a very violent figure*) You hear me? (*He suddenly realizes what he is doing—and abruptly relaxes, turns away, and reaches for a drink bottle*)

Ann *That* is going to do your blood pressure a whole lot of good.

Terry hesitates, then puts the bottle down

Terry You're right. Trouble with you is, Ann, you're *always* bloody right. (*He wags his finger*) Bad habit in a woman. A woman should at least pretend some weaknesses. You mark my words—when Mr Right comes along one day and . . . (*He stops, realizing what he has said*) Ann, I'm sorry. Levity in the worst possible taste. You and Steve . . . (*To Jenny*). And your old man languishing in a cell somewhere . . .

Ann (*over-riding him*) Terry! (*He stares at her*) Just do us all a favour and keep quiet.

Terry nods miserably and turns away

The door suddenly slams open and Andy enters

They all stare at him

Andy (*with forced humour, a humour he does not really feel*) I got parolled. Good behaviour!

Jenny They let you go?

Andy Yes. Travesty of Justice, isn't it?

Jenny Where's Peter?

Andy They *didn't* let him go. I hoped I'd find you all here—the cosy conspirators . . .

Act III, Scene 1 41

Jenny But what about Peter—is he . . . ?
Andy (*snarling*) Just let me have my say, lady!
Terry Now look here . . .
Andy And you keep quiet, too! Your little parlour game back-fired, didn't it? You couldn't just bring me in, say "there's been a murder, and can you help?" No, that would've been too direct—instead you had to try and stick the whole shebang on to my shoulders. Be convenient if it'd worked, wouldn't it? Because I'm not like you. Be nice that—to think it was *my* kind—and not yours that killed those two people, wouldn't it . . . ?
Terry (*stumbling*) We—just thought—we hoped . . .
Andy I know what you bloody well *hoped*. But I've got an alibi, see? I'm clever like that. You have to be—living rough and free you have to have an alibi for everything—so they couldn't prove a thing. (*He regards them*) All of a kind. You're like her—like she was. Maggie. Too much education and not enough sense. (*He suddenly calms down, becomes almost his old self again*) Well, I've had my say. Just didn't want you to think you were getting away with anything. (*He moves to open the door, then pauses*) Oh—now for the good news. They're holding your husband —probably for ever—you see, they just charged him with the murder of Maggie Miller!

Andy exits

Jenny reacts

Terry The cheap little bastard. I should have . . . !

Ann moves to Jenny

Ann Jenny . . .
Terry We'll get a damned good lawyer—the best.
Jenny (*shaking her head*) The police don't bring a charge unless they're sure.
Terry Well, perhaps Flewin was lying. I wouldn't put it past him to . . .

Terry is cut short as the telephone starts to ring. He turns to stare at it. It rings and rings

Ann Well, answer it!
Terry What's the point. It'll be for Maggie—and Maggie's gone.
Ann Answer it—it might be the police about Peter.

Terry moves over to pick up the telephone

Terry (*into the telephone*) Hello? . . . Yes, speaking as a matter of fact. (*To the others*) It *is* the police. Yes. . . . Yes. . . . *What!*

There is a dramatic change in Terry—he is very shocked. Jenny and Ann turn towards him

N—now wait a minute—that can't be . . . I—I mean, people just don't do that—do they? . . . Well, yes, I'll tell her—I'll tell her right away.

(*He drops the telephone back on the receiver—and stands there, very shocked still, for a long moment*)

Ann Well for God's sake—what is it?
Terry It's Peter . . .
Jenny Peter?

Terry nods vaguely, but still he does not move

Terry (*anguished*) Why—why did he have to do that? Oh God, *why!*
Jenny What is it—what's happened to Peter?
Terry They've taken him to hospital—artificial respiration, they said . . .
Ann Why, Terry? What's happened!?
Terry (*finally turning to them*) The poor bloody fool just hanged himself!

Ann is frozen by the news, and so too is Jenny for a moment—but then she lets out an awful cry of anguish, as—

the CURTAIN *falls*

SCENE 2

The same. About two hours later

The room is becoming shadowy with the onset of dusk

The first bedroom door opens and Ann enters. She is carrying the large suitcase we saw her arrive with. She descends the stairs to the main area—looks around and then—she has a tidy mind—she sees Terry's unfinished drink. She puts down her suitcase, then moves to tidy away the drinks bottle. As she puts the bottle in the tall cupboard, she is again reminded of what this cupboard once held. She takes the glass and moves to the sink to wash it up. As she does this she sees, where it has lain forgotten, the note Maggie left. She picks it up

Ann (*reading the card*) "Darling. Have just popped into the village to pick up the cake. Make yourself at . . ." (*She cannot continue*) Oh, Maggie! Maggie! (*She holds the card to her for a moment, then puts it down again. Getting control of herself, she turns to move back towards her suitcase. But this time she steps on the fragments of the shattered figurine. She reacts and gets a dustpan and brush. She sweeps up the fragments, then moves to put them in the waste-bin. She stops, regards the fragments, and finally does not dispose of them. Instead she carefully pours the fragments on to a table and touches them with her hands—she is coming to a decision. She moves to the telephone, finds the telephone directory, thumbs through it, then dials a number*)

A slight pause

(*Into the telephone*) Harringhams? Could you put me through to your porcelain department, please? . . . Thank you.

Act III, Scene 2   43

As Ann waits—suddenly, startlingly, the front door bursts open to the wind. She looks at the door, seems about to move to close it, but at this moment someone speaks on the telephone

(*Into the telephone*) Oh, hello? Porcelain?

The open door is forgotten now, and as Ann speaks we see Terry enter and stand in the open doorway

(*Into the telephone*) I wonder if you can help me? About a week ago you had a figurine in your window. About a foot high—white porcelain—a woman—sort of *art nouveau*-ish. . . . Yes, that's the one. Well, I wondered if. . . It was the only one in stock, and it's sold? Well, that's marvellous! . . . No, no, you see I'm trying to find out who bought it. Can you help me? . . . The manager? . . . Well, when will he be back? . . . I see. Well, do you think you could ask him to call me with the information as soon as he gets back? . . . Ann Marsh. Amerhill two-two-one. . . . Yes, thank you. . . . Yes, I'll wait for his call. (*She hangs up*) I'll wait.

Behind her, Terry pushes the door shut with a fairly loud bang. Ann spins round to see him

Terry! Where's Jenny?
Terry Left her at the hospital.
Ann And Peter—is he . . . ?
Terry (*interjecting*) He's alive. Just. He'll pull through—but he'll probably be six inches taller. Bloody fool. What did he want to have to do that for? Try and top himself—why did he have to go and do that?

A slight pause. Ann regards him

Ann I didn't hear your car.
Terry Probably because I didn't bring it. (*He turns to face her*) Left it at the hospital for Jenny. She ought to be along here soon. (*Pacing away, muttering*) I couldn't stand being around that place any longer.
Ann How did you get back here then?
Terry I walked. (*He moves to the telephone*)
Ann Walked?
Terry (*turning back to Ann*) Walked! I *can* still do it you know—my legs haven't atrophied! Anyway—it's probably good for my blood pressure!
Ann I'm sorry—it's just—well—it's a long way.
Terry I needed a long way. Perspective. Needed to get—certain things straight in my mind.

Ann regards him—he is in a remote, strange mood

Ann Well, I'll be leaving soon—was just getting my things together.
Terry (*vaguely*) Don't mind me.

Ann hesitates for the barest moment—and then she ascends the stairs to exit into the first bedroom door. She leaves the door open behind her

Terry remains still for a moment—then he begins to wander around the area. His actions could be interpreted as those of a man reliving poignant memories—or those of a killer reliving the crime. He moves to the cupboard that held Maggie's body, then to the place where the sword once was, moves on, pauses by the knife rack, and then moves towards the table that bears the fragments. As he does this he starts to whistle—not a tune, just vague snatches of whistling, tuneless whistling

>Ann enters from the first bedroom—and remains on the gallery, rooted there, holding the top-coat she went to collect, and staring down at Terry who is whistling—tunelessly

Terry discards the figurine fragments and his hand lightly touches the telephone—he might be about to disable it—he might be about to make a call—he might just be physically doodling. We will never know—for at this moment we hear the sports car drive up and stop. Terry reacts—and then becomes aware of Ann on the stairs

>(*In a flat monotone*) Jenny. (*He opens the door*)

>*Jenny enters. She moves right past Terry and sits down—she seems utterly drained of emotion*

Terry closes the door and looks meaningly at Ann. Ann quickly descends the stairs now and moves to Jenny

Ann (*softly*) Jenny . . .

Jenny does not seem to hear. Ann touches her shoulder. Jenny looks up and seems to be seeing Ann for the first time

>(*gently*) Thank God Peter's all right.
Jenny All right? There's a detective beside his bed waiting to take him away as soon as he recovers! As far as they're concerned that wraps it up—an attempt at suicide is as good as a signed confession! (*She removes her distinctive coat and places it in some prominent position*)
Terry Easy on, old girl.
Ann Shall I make you some tea?
Jenny I don't know—I suppose so.

Ann nods, smiles encouragingly, then moves away to start making tea

Ann Terry?

Before Terry can say whether he wants tea or not, the telephone rings. Terry reacts

Terry I've got to go. (*He moves rapidly to the door*)

Ann is torn between him and the ringing telephone for a moment

Ann But, Terry . . .
Terry (*over-riding her*) I'll see you.

>*Terry exits*

Ann gazes after him, then moves to pick up the telephone. Jenny does not move—just sits staring at her hands, apparently unaware of the telephone

Act III, Scene 2   45

Ann (*into the telephone*) Hello? No, I'm sorry, Maggie isn't here any more. . . . No. . . . No, she just isn't here.

Ann hangs up. We hear Terry's sports car start up and move away. Ann gazes at the door as the sound of the car recedes

I think he loved Maggie—really loved her.

Jenny (*as though awakening from a daze, lifting her head*) Maggie?

Suddenly, startlingly, the door bursts open again. Jenny rises and quickly moves to close it. She remains by the door for a moment

In Switzerland there's a special wind that blows. A warm, blustery wind.

Ann The Föhn-Wind.

Jenny That's it, that's what they call it. And in France it's the Mistral—and somewhere else it's the Sirocco. A blustery wind—like this one. A wind that sends people mad.

Jenny moves close to Ann—and takes down a large carving-knife from the rack near the sink—she toys with it—then Ann glances at her

Can I give you a hand?

Ann Not with that. Not unless you want a sandwich or something?

Jenny No . . . (*She regards the big knife she holds, as though seeing it for the first time*) No. (*Suddenly, startlingly, she raises the knife high and plunges it into the draining-board. It remains impaled there. Then she turns and meanders away across the area*) A wind that sends you mad. It does you know. It really does—even the authorities recognize it. If you commit a crime in Switzerland during the Föhn-Wind, the sentence is reduced. Even murder. They treat you—very leniently. It's like a woman murdering her child just after she's given birth to it. They don't even call it murder—they call it—something else . . . ?

Ann Infanticide.

Jenny Infanticide. Not murder at all—because the woman is mentally disturbed at the time. (*Sharper*) Not *insane* you understand? Just—mentally disturbed—as she would be if she was being buffeted by a big blustery wind all day. Did you know that Maggie was pregnant?

Ann What!

Jenny (*nodding*) One of the detectives told me. The autopsy you see. She was three months pregnant. (*Far away*) But I already knew, of course.

Ann Maggie told you?

Jenny (*starting*) No. No, no. I—guessed. The way she looked. Women get that—special look. (*She meanders away again*) Maggie was pregnant. Imagine what play she would have made of that!

Ann Jenny—Maggie is *dead*!

Jenny stares at Ann blankly

Jenny Yes. Yes, she is, isn't she. She can't hurt us any more.

There is a knock at the door. Ann opens it

> Andy enters, looks at her, then moves straight across the area to pick up the painting. He then turns to regard Ann and Jenny

Andy I was never paid for it. It's mine.
Ann All right—take it and go.

Andy stops, starts to move, then stops

Andy It was just an excuse. I've been hanging around until *he* left.
Ann Who?
Andy Him—Dexter or whatever his name is. (*He hesitates*) It's not like me to blow my top like that. Not to women. I'm renowned for my courtly manners. It was him—*he* was the one I wanted to hit back at. I had to include you too because—because you were here and I wasn't thinking straight. Look, I'm *trying* to apologize!
Ann (*wearily*) Accepted.

Andy moves to stand over Jenny

Andy I heard about your husband and what he tried to do and—well, I hope he gets off, that's all.

Jenny does not even look at him. Andy looks at Ann

Anything I can do to help?
Ann No.

Andy regards Jenny, then becomes aware of the painting he still holds. He turns to Ann

Andy Look, would you like to have this? Free, gratis, jump in quick because Andy Flewin rarely gives anything away!
Ann No thank you.
Andy Spoken like a true critic. (*He regards the painting at arm's length*) See what you mean though—badly painted, no colour sense and—it's of her. Listen, I meant what I said—about being sorry. 'Specially you. I don't think you're like the others. (*A pause. He again regards Jenny*) Well. (*He moves to the door, opens it, and again regards the painting*) I think I'll burn it.

Andy exits

A pause. Ann continues making tea, watching Jenny closely. She hands her a cup of tea. Jenny says nothing, listlessly stirs her tea. Ann watches her

Ann Jenny, what are you going to do?
Jenny Do?
Ann Until things are—well—sorted out with Peter. You're not going to stay alone, are you?
Jenny Alone?
Ann Do you have relatives, friends—someone nearby you could stay with?
Jenny No.
Ann Then why don't you come back to town with me?

Jenny turns to stare at Ann

Ann I have a spare room—you're welcome to it. I just don't think you should be alone—not now . . .

Act III, Scene 2

Jenny I never actually liked Maggie. Never. (*She looks at Ann*) Go back with you? Why? So that you can keep an eye on me—so you know where I am!
Ann You know that's not the reason!
Jenny I'm sorry. Yes, perhaps it would be a good idea—to come home with you.
Ann (*picking up her suitcase*) That's settled then—we'll get a cab—nip over to your place and pick up whatever you want and then . . . Oh!

Jenny looks at Ann, who puts her suitcase down again

Forgot my purse. (*She starts to ascend the stairs*) Won't be a moment. You can be phoning for a cab.

Ann exits into the first bedroom

Jenny remains utterly still for a moment then she looks at the telephone. Finally she rises from her chair and moves to it. She reaches the telephone, hesitates—and at this moment the telephone rings. It rings only once, because she picks it up

Jenny (*into the telephone*) Hello? . . . Oh, yes—Harringhams. . . . (*She listens—then looks towards the bedroom*) No, but I can take a message. . . . The figurine? . . . I see. . . . Yes. . . . Yes, I'll tell her. . . . Thank you. Good-bye.

While speaking, Jenny turns to face upstage. She quietly replaces the receiver and remains for a long moment, utterly still. Then she picks up some of the fragments of the figurine from the table and lets them trickle through her fingers and fall back on the table. Then she turns, again looks up the stairs towards the bedroom, and moves away to the sink unit, to where the big knife is still impaled in the draining-board. She grips it and pulls it from the draining-board

Ann enters from the first bedroom door, carrying a small purse

Jenny spins round, concealing the knife behind her back

Ann (*descending the stairs*) It had slipped down behind the bed. (*She steps off the stairs—moves to her suitcase and glances at Jenny*) Did I hear the phone just now?
Jenny Why—were you expecting a call?
Ann (*shrugging*) Sort of—but it's something I can easily check up on later.
Jenny No, there was no call.
Ann What about the cab?
Jenny Cab? Oh, yes, it's on its way.
Ann (*picking up her suitcase*) Fancy a walk—we could meet it half way?
Jenny I'm not going with you after all.
Ann Oh, Jenny . . .
Jenny Or rather—you'll be staying here with me.

Jenny produces the knife from behind her back. Ann stares at it and her for a long moment, then looks at the telephone

Ann I *did* hear the phone. Harringhams returned my call, didn't they? So it was you who bought the figurine. And it was you who killed Maggie and Steve. And now what Jenny? Kill me?
Jenny Kill you? I don't want to kill you, Ann—I want to persuade you. Convince you.
Ann Convince?
Jenny (*staring at her*) You don't know, do you? You really don't have any idea . . .
Ann Idea of what . . . ?
Jenny Yes. Harringhams called and yes, they told me who bought the figurine. It was *you*! Ann Marsh! It was *your* present to Maggie!
Ann Mine? How could it be mine?

We are not sure whether Jenny is playing a devious game or not

Jenny You picked it up from Harringhams *the day before yesterday*—you made a special trip to collect it because you wanted to give it to your friend *that* day! They remember you saying that.
Ann The day *before* yesterday? That's impossible—I didn't arrive here until yesterday.
Jenny Oh, but you did.

Ann stares at her

Ann Persuade me? Convince me? Assume *your* guilt, is that your plan? Well, it isn't going to work. (*She goes towards the telephone*) I'll call Harringhams. *I'll* get the truth . . .
Jenny (*intervening between Ann and the telephone*) Ann. *Ann!* Don't you see? (*She picks up the note, flourishes it*) *This* note. It *was* meant for you! It was *always* meant for you! It was waiting for you when you arrived here *the day before yesterday*!

Ann stares at her

But you don't remember, do you?
Ann I most certainly do not!

Both Ann and Jenny talk with utter conviction—it is impossible to pick out which one is lying

Jenny Of course, you wouldn't remember . . .
Ann Because it's a pack of lies . . .
Jenny Because of the crash! The air crash! That was bad, wasn't it, Ann? Very bad. You were in shock—in a coma for weeks—*and when you came out of it you didn't remember any part of it!*

Ann is shaken, unsure for the first time

You see, Ann—it's happened to you before. Something awful—terrible—and then your mind blotting it out—because it's too painful to remember!
Ann No.

Act III, Scene 2   49

Jenny Yes, Ann. *Yes.*
Ann That I came here the day *before* yesterday . . . ?
Jenny *That* day.
Ann No.
Jenny *That* day—that terrible day. What happened? You let yourself in, put Maggie's present on the table there—and then Maggie came down the stairs—and then you heard Steve's voice—from the bedroom—and suddenly you realized that Steve and Maggie . . . Something snapped in your mind and then—it happened . . .
Ann No. *No!* (*She rounds on Jenny, clutching at straws*) The woman who took the taxi from here that night—that was Maggie . . .
Jenny It was *you.*
Ann But the taxi driver—Terry said . . .
Jenny Terry said he *described* Maggie to the taxi driver—how? Slim, attractive? That would fit you, Ann.
Ann And you, too.
Jenny Ann.
Ann (*over-riding her*) And the dress, *my* dress, what was it you said when you first saw it? "I saw the self-same dress in Harringhams!" When, Jenny? When were you in Harringhams? And why were you there? To buy Maggie's birthday present . . . ?
Jenny No, Ann—listen to me . . .
Ann (*over-riding her*) No, *you listen to me!* There's one other thing been back of my mind and bothering me. The drink—those crates of bubbly? Yesterday I asked about the drink for the party, and *you* said it had been *delivered the day before.* Now, how could you have known that? How could you have known if you hadn't been here?
Jenny Because—because the delivery man called at my house *first.* He told me he was dropping the stuff off at Maggie's.

Ann stares at her

You were the woman who took that cab from here, Ann. And before you left, you put the key back—"force of habit"—then, the next day, you turned up here again—as though nothing had happened—*not knowing anything had happened.* And you went through the whole charade again.

Ann No, I'd remember. I would remember.
Jenny Tell me about the air-crash, Ann! Just give me one fragment—one incident that you can recall. Convince *me!*
Ann (*softly*) Convince . . . ?
Jenny What happened here is still locked away in your mind somewhere. From the first moment you came here—stepped through that door, saw Maggie, heard Steve's voice . . . "Come back to bed, Maggie".
Ann The one thing you dreaded to hear.
Jenny No, not me—*you*—I can see the look on Maggie's face—taunting you . . .
Ann Taunting *you*, Jenny. With what—Peter's child? And suddenly the sword is in your hand, and you're plunging it into her. And then—the man

who betrayed you—you creep up the stairs—it's dark up there, you see a man, think it's Peter and . . .

Jenny Stop it! Stop it! And force yourself to remember the truth, Ann—the truth! After it's over comes the panic—you must get away—take Maggie's car—drive away——

Ann —*along the back road*—that leads to *your* house, Jenny.

Jenny It's also a short cut to the main road—that's why you took it—but then the car gets stuck in the mud—won't move. You run back here, but you're calmer now—you can think more clearly. Drag Maggie's body out of sight, into the cupboard. Then phone for a cab—drive away, and put it out of your mind for ever.

Ann stares at her

Ann A very graphic description. The description of an *eye witness*!

Jenny No!

Ann It *was* you. You did it and now you're trying to make me believe that I . . .

Jenny (*interjecting*) I'm trying to make you remember!

They regard each other

There's only one way to find out the truth. One only way. (*She begins a slow advance towards Ann—still, quite unconsciously, holding the knife*) Reconstruct. Relive the whole thing, thought for thought, word for word, relive the whole thing . . .

CURTAIN

SCENE 3

The same. Monday morning, a fine, bright day

The set is empty. Terry's hand appears at the transom and feels for the key. The door is opened, and Terry enters. He wears an airline captain's uniform. He closes the door, looks around, then begins to search around the place. As he searches, he whistles faintly, tunelessly. His search eventually takes him near to the foot of the stairs, and suddenly a small sound from above alerts him. He looks up the stairs

Terry Hello? Anyone here? Hello?

Silence. He shrugs, continues searching, and then reacts as the upstairs bedroom door opens. Terry freezes, watches and waits

Ann enters from the first bedroom, carrying her week-end case. She descends the stairs casually, without furtiveness

Terry makes his presence known as she reaches the bottom of the stairs

Ann.

Act III, Scene 3   51

Ann Terry! (*Startled, she drops her case*)
Terry Here! Sorry, old girl . . . (*He hastens to pick up her case*)
Ann Terry, for God's sake . . .
Terry Didn't mean to frighten you.
Ann Well, you certainly did.
Terry Sorry. Sorry.
Ann What are you doing here, anyway?
Terry About to ask you the same thing.
Ann Where's Jenny?
Terry Eh? How should I know?
Ann You didn't see her on your way here?
Terry Not a soul. Why?
Ann (*almost to herself*) Perhaps she went home, then.
Terry I thought everyone left here ages ago.
Ann I meant to. I was going to. And then she—she scared me.
Terry Jenny did?
Ann Yes. Well, perhaps not scared so much as—disturbed . . .
Terry What do you mean, she scared you?
Ann I shouldn't say. Not without positive proof.
Terry Proof of what? Ann?
Ann You asked me what I'm still doing here—well, I'm humouring Jenny.
Terry Humouring?
Ann Terry, why are you here, why have you come back?
Terry Me? Well I—er—I left my lighter somewhere and . . .
Ann Lighter?
Terry The one Maggie gave me; I wouldn't want to lose that, not now; she paid a small fortune for it at Harringhams and . . . Ah! (*He sees and homes in on the lighter. He picks it up and clicks it triumphantly*) You see? (*He regards her*) This business about "humouring" Jenny . . . ?
Ann No, I have no right . . .
Terry Come on, I want to know. Is it about Steve and Maggie? If it is then I have a *right* to know. *Ann!*
Ann It's all so mixed up, so confused. You're sure you didn't see her on your way here?
Terry Quite, quite sure.

He watches as Ann moves to open the front door and stare out

Ann Then she *did* go home. Or she's out there somewhere—hiding . . . (*The thought is too much; she firmly closes the door and turns to Terry*) Terry, it was her. She did it.
Terry What! D'you mean she confessed, she told you that? We're in the clear, is that what you're saying?
Ann Not exactly.
Terry Then dammit, what *are* you saying? *What* did she tell you!?

Ann paces away, then stops as she sees and picks up Jenny's distinctive coat, which is in a place of concealment. She reacts

Ann This is her coat!

Terry Eh?
Ann Jenny's coat. So she must still be around. Somewhere in the house! (*She turns to look up the stairs*) Not upstairs, I would have seen her. But . . . (*She turns to look at the box-room door*)

Terry reacts, then strides over to open the door, look inside the room, and then firmly close the door again

Terry Empty.

Ann turns to stare at the front door, still holding Jenny's coat

Ann She *is* outside. I know it. She's outside, listening—watching us—and waiting. Waiting for the right moment . . .
Terry (*interjecting*) Ann, this is nonsense. (*He strides over to open the door—there is nothing beyond*) Nonsense—or she's scared you rotten. But how? Why?

Ann merely stares at him. He firmly closes the door

Very well, I'll lock the door. (*He pushes the bolt home*) There. The door is firmly bolted, and we're quite alone now, Ann. Just you and me. Now tell me what you know—or what you think you know.

Ann regards him, then seems to wilt or relax a little

Ann Terry, I'm sorry. Sorry.
Terry Come on, old girl, tell Terry everything. Tell Uncle Terry, and he'll know what to do.
Ann It was Jenny. She did it.
Terry Yes, you said that, but what makes you think it's true? What have you found out? Eh? Eh?
Ann Soon after you left we got to talking. She said—so many strange things. That's when I decided to go along with her. She was so frightening, so scarey, the only safe thing I *could* do was go along with her!
Terry Go along where?
Ann It was her idea—to reconstruct the whole thing, go back and relive the whole of that terrible day before yesterday—the day we arrived here so happily—not knowing—not suspecting that Steve and Maggie were . . . (*She starts to break*) She's dangerous, Terry, dangerous because she's so lucid. She tried to make me believe that *I—that I* . . . !

Ann half collapses against Terry—he pats and consoles her

Terry You need a drink. We both do.

He leaves her, so that she remains facing out front, as he crosses to the big cupboard. He reaches it, then stops

The day before yesterday?
Ann Yes. Friday.
Terry The day before . . .? What day do you think it is now, then?
Ann It's Sunday, of course.
Terry You *do* need a drink. (*He turns back to the cupboard*) You're in

Act III, Scene 3   53

worse shape than I thought. Sunday? Today is *Monday*! You've lost a whole day, old girl. Mind you, with what's been going on here it's no wonder. But a whole day! Any idea where you've been, what you might have been up to in that time . . . ?

As Terry talks he opens the cupboard—and reacts. He lets the door swing wider, so that we can see, wedged into the cupboard, Jenny's body. He stares at it as Ann speaks

Ann I don't remember. I don't remember. I don't remember.

CURTAIN

FURNITURE AND PROPERTY LIST

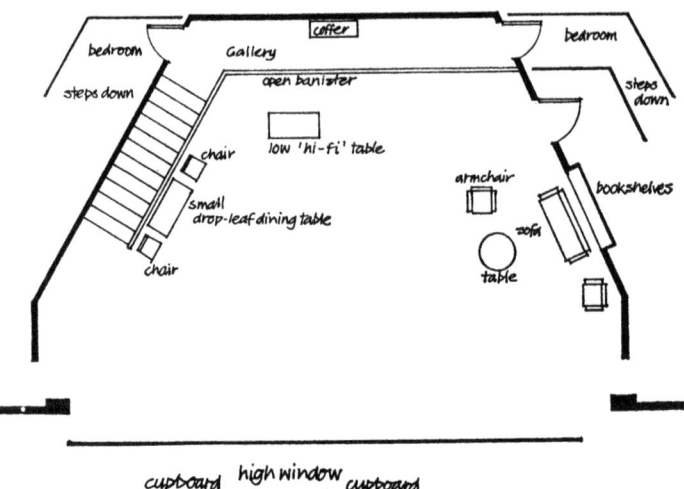

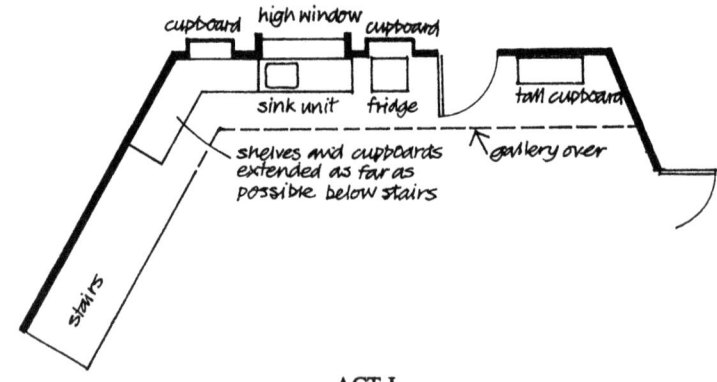

ACT I

On stage: Chesterfield. *On it:* cushions
2 armchairs. *On them:* cushions
Coffee table. *On it:* ashtray with long cigarette-end
Small dining-table. *On it:* telephone, directory
2 small chairs with soft-cushioned seats
Small pedestal. *On it:* pot plant, figurine
Table. *On it:* Hi-fi outfit, records. Tape-recorder with large written card propped against it
Tall, two-door cupboard. *Right-hand section:* shelves with bottles of whisky, gin, brandy, champagne (2), other drinks, assorted glasses, foodstuffs including packet of tea, tin of biscuits, birthday cake with candles. *Left-hand section:* bare, no shelves
Bookcase with books
Kitchen sink (practical) with wooden draining-board. *On it:* cloths and various kitchen utensils. *Beside it:* rack containing bric-à-brac and large kitchen knife. *Under it:* dustpan, brush, waste bin

Shock! 55

	Kitchen cupboards, drawers and shelves. *In or on them:* electric kettle, teapot, plates, cups, saucers, jugs, sugar bowl, cutlery, large empty tea tin
	Refrigerator. *In it:* tonic water bottles, wrapped barbecue steaks, milk
	On landing: large coffer. *In it:* ceramic head of woman, with card attached
	On wall at top of stairs: Chinese wind chime
	On walls and round room generally: various foreign *objets d'art*, including bloodstained Samurai sword wedged against a beam
	On main door: knocker (outside), bolt (inside), large keyhole
	Carpet
	Staircarpet
Off-stage:	Week-end case (**Ann**)
	Parcel with party dress and hanger (**Ann**)
	"Birthday" parcels (**Terry**)
	Wrapped painting of Maggie, with cord (**Andy**)
	Tool box with hammer, nails, large black pencil (**Andy**)
Personal:	**Peter:** large doorkey
	Jenny: cigarettes, lighter

ACT II

Personal:	**Peter:** cigarettes, lighter

ACT III
Scene 1

Strike:	All used cups, saucers, glasses
	Birthday cake
	Picture wrapping
	Tape-recorder
	Samurai sword
Set:	All cupboard and closet doors open
	Box-room door open
	Furniture, ornaments, etc., moved around
	Fingerprint "dust" on furniture, door-knobs, etc.
	Maggie painting near foot of stairs
	Figurine in prominent position on dining-table

Scene 2

Off stage:	Purse (**Ann**)

Scene 3

Strike:	Used tea-things
Set:	Check **Terry's** lighter
	Check position of **Jenny's** coat
Off stage:	Week-end case (**Ann**)

LIGHTING PLOT

Property fittings required: wall brackets or pendant, plug for electric kettle
Interior. A living-room-kitchen-gallery. The same scene throughout

ACT I. Late afternoon

To open: General effect of late sunshine

Cue 1   As Act opens   (Page 1)
          Start very slow fade, lasting throughout Act, to
          shadowy dusk

ACT II. Late afternoon, at dusk

To open: As close of Act I

Cue 2   **Jenny** switches on lights   (Page 19)
          Snap on practicals and full interior lighting

ACT III, SCENE 1.   Late afternoon

To open: As Act I

No cues

ACT III, SCENE 2.   Late afternoon

To open: Slightly darker than close of previous scene

Cue 3   As Scene opens   (Page 42)
          Slow fade to dusk

ACT III, SCENE 3.   Morning

To open: General effect of bright sunshine

No cues

EFFECTS PLOT

ACT I

Cue 1	**Peter** shuts coffer	(Page 2)
	Pause, then sound of taxi approaching, stopping, door opening and closing	
Cue 2	**Ann:** "I can manage."	(Page 2)
	Taxi starts up and leaves	
Cue 3	**Ann** starts tape-recorder	(Page 6)
	Tape-recorder: pleasant music	
Cue 4	**Ann:** ". . . firmly on the ground."	(Page 7)
	Sports car approaches, horn blowing, and skids to a stop	
Cue 5	**Terry** exits	(Page 8)
	Pause, then sports car drives away	
Cue 6	**Andy:** "I'm a fast worker."	(Page 12)
	Sports car arrives and stops	
Cue 7	**Terry** exits	(Page 15)
	Pause, then sports car drives away	
Cue 8	**Jenny** and **Ann** regard painting	(Page 16)
	Sports car arrives and stops	
Cue 9	**Terry** exits	(Page 16)
	Pause, then sports car drives away	
Cue 10	**Ann** starts tape-recorder	(Page 17)
	Tape-recorder: music, then added laughter, love-making sounds, voices, etc., Chinese chime, door-slam, silence	

ACT II

Cue 11	**Ann** moves to cover Steve with dress	(Page 20)
	Tape-recorder: door-slam, movements, voices, Chinese chime, footsteps, metallic sound, a crash	
Cue 12	**Ann** resets tape-recorder and starts it	(Page 20)
	Tape-recorder: high-speed noise, then tuneless whistling	
Cue 13	**Jenny** resets tape-recorder and starts it	(Page 23)
	Tape-recorder: high-speed noise, followed by tuneless whistling: repeat when she restarts tape-recorder two speeches later	
Cue 14	**Ann** starts tape-recorder	(Page 26)
	Tape-recorder: tuneless whistling	
Cue 15	**Jenny:** "I don't mind going . . ."	(Page 27)
	Sports car arrives and stops; horn sounds	
Cue 16	**Ann** starts recorder	(Page 29)
	Tape-recorder: voices, metallic sound, crash	
Cue 17	**Terry:** "—where is Maggie?"	(Page 31)
	Telephone rings	
Cue 18	**Terry** resets and starts tape-recorder	(Page 33)
	Tape-recorder: silence, music, love-making, voices	

ACT III
Scene 1

Cue 19	**Ann** examines figurine *Sports car drives up and stops*	(Page 37)
Cue 20	**Terry**: ". . . wouldn't put it past him to . . ." *Telephone rings*	(Page 41)

Scene 2

Cue 21	**Ann** waits at telephone *Wind bursts door open*	(Page 43)
Cue 22	**Ann** watches **Terry** *Sports car drives up and stops*	(Page 44)
Cue 23	**Ann**: "Terry?" *Telephone rings*	(Page 44)
Cue 24	**Ann**: ". . . she just isn't here." *Sports car drives away*	(Page 45)
Cue 25	**Jenny**: "Maggie?" *Wind bursts door open*	(Page 45)
Cue 26	**Jenny** hesitates by telephone *Telephone rings*	(Page 47)

Scene 3

No cues

MADE AND PRINTED IN GREAT BRITAIN BY
LATIMER TREND & COMPANY LTD PLYMOUTH
MADE IN ENGLAND

www.ingramcontent.com/pod-product-compliance
Ingram Content Group UK Ltd.
Pitfield, Milton Keynes, MK11 3LW, UK
UKHW021847210426
5322IPUK00022B/521